Wounded but not Dead

Transfixus sed non Mortuus

Mary Walsh

Wounded but not Dead

Copyright © 2019
Mary Walsh

marywalshwrites.com

Wounded but not Dead

Discover other books by Mary Walsh

The Curse of Jean Lafitte
Knights of the Corporate Round Table
American Posse
Memories of 9/11
Plenty of Fish in the Ocean State
Once Upon a Time in Chicago
His Second Chance
Where or When
Fine Spirits Served Here
You Deserve Better
Life Lessons for my Kids
Dragon Slayer
Catch a Break
Stable of Studs

This book is dedicated to anyone who has any type of major surgery or illness.

Keep moving forward. You can do it!

Chapter 1

Inches and Seconds

Five minutes changed my life forever. 300 seconds. A blink of my existence in life and my world altered forever.

At 7:10 a.m. on Thursday, October 4, 2018, I woke my daughter, Anita, before I headed to work.

"Why are you leaving early today?" she asked me, rubbing sleepy eyes. "My alarm hasn't gone off yet. How come you're leaving now?" She knew I rarely left for work before 7:15 when I made sure she was awake before she headed to high school. Like any typical teenager, she liked sleeping in as long as possible.

"I finished getting ready a little bit sooner today, so I'm going to work," I told her. "I'll see you after field hockey practice today." After kissing her on the forehead, I headed out the door and hopped in my car.

The weather, in the low 70s, was warm for early October in south-central Pennsylvania. By this time of the year, we succumbed to wearing light jackets and sweaters. But not that day. I wore a long sleeve black top and a long boho pink and black printed skirt that I had purchased two weeks earlier. Black open-toed stack heeled sandals were on my feet.

We lived in Mechanicsburg, ten miles west of the capital city of Harrisburg. I poked along Main Street at 25 miles per hour, passing the 100-year-old ice cream shop, the hardware store where the Mayor did most of his business, and the new cupcakery. The community hadn't changed much in over a century. Every third Thursday in June, our town hosted Jubilee Day, the largest one-day street festival on the East Coast. That might not sound like much, but it is a time-honored tradition for our close-knit community. Over 70,000 people invaded our tranquil town every year.

After winding my way a few blocks along Main Street, I found myself on the main road heading out of the historic downtown section. Kids skipped along the sidewalk on their way to school. Tall oaks blasted the avenue with rich orange, yellow, and brown hues. Many houses and shops were decorated with pumpkins and hay bales for the upcoming Halloween parade.

A block later, as I navigated an upcoming S-curve in the road, a small commercial flatbed truck headed toward me in the oncoming lane. The truck was carrying a load of granite slabs in an A-frame. When I took another quick look, the strappings on the side of the truck snapped.

Holy crap it's coming off!

I watched in slow motion as the granite fell off the side of the truck. In a split-second reaction, I purposely swerved to the right, hoping to get out of the way of rogue granite.

A chunk of granite hit the lower section of my 2015 Honda CR-V with a large bang, causing the car to jerk.

Then everything went black into a cloud of dust.

My sight was blocked and my car swerved a few times. I clenched the steering wheel, trying in vain to control my deranged car. After what seemed like fifteen or twenty seconds in the raging dark, my car finally came to a stop.

This vehicle has been in an accident... This vehicle has been in an accident... robotically echoed through my car.

The dust fog settled and I heaved a sigh of relief. No broken glass and I wasn't bleeding. Maybe the damage to my car was as good as I felt? Shaken up, but still intact. I had never been in a major car accident before, so I was unsure what to expect.

A moment later, a dark-haired man approached the outside of my vehicle. Where did he come from?

"Do you want me to get you out?" he called to me through the window.

"Yes!" I answered, fearing that my car could still catch on fire, regardless of my potential injuries and car damage.

He attempted to open my driver's side door, but it was jammed shut. Still fearful of impending fire, I raced to unbuckle my seatbelt. My airbags had not deployed, so my path to the passenger side door was clear. Adrenaline pushed me to help myself. I hoisted myself up over the center console and opened the passenger door to the dark-haired man.

In the few seconds that it took me to move myself, two other men joined the first man and all three of them quickly pulled me out of my car.

"Get her out now! Get her out! Now!" the one man yelled to the others.

They gingerly carried me to a small patch of grass about 20 feet away from my car. Not knowing the extent of any injuries I might have, they laid me on my side.

One of the men asked me, "Is anyone else in the car?"

"No," I replied. "Just me."

"What's your name?" he asked me. "Do you have any info on you?"

"Mary... My purse.... in the front seat," I gasped, my heart still racing from being in the accident. I didn't feel injured but was still in shock from the trauma of being tossed around like a rag doll.

As he ran over to my car to retrieve my belongings, the other two men kneeled on the grass next to me.

I gazed over the shoulder of the one man, and finally focused on my car behind him.

"Is that... my car?" I knew the answer but still begged the question.

My mouth fell open as I cocked my head to the side in stupefaction.

The entire driver's side front tire of my car was sliced off, like taking a knife to a tomato. The car had jumped the curb in reverse and came to rest against a telephone pole at a 45-degree angle.

How did I not feel any of this moments earlier?

How on earth did I come out unscathed?

Why did my airbags not deploy?

And, knowing me, if my good Samaritans were not around, I would have tried to get out of the car myself. No wonder they were in a rush to get me out. They feared that my car might collapse to the ground.

The second man returned with my purse and laid it next to me. "I'm an off-duty police officer," he said. "I'll call for an ambulance."

"Okay, thank you," I replied while lying on my side.

And then I shrieked in pain.

The other two men scrambled to help me, putting a rolled-up jacket under my head and a found blanket over my torso. The warm weather didn't make a difference.

"My back," I puffed out. "It hurts."

They delicately rolled me to my back to alleviate some pain. One of the men pulled my cell phone out of my purse. "Who can I call?" he asked me.

"Call my dad," I sputtered. "Call my dad."

While he was scrolling through my contacts, I overheard the off-duty police officer say into his phone, "Yes, we have a late 20s, early 30s white female with unidentified injuries..."

"No, no, no... " I corrected him. "I'm 45." Under normal circumstances, I would have been flattered. Any potential medical personnel would need to know my exact age.

The man who held my phone finally reached my dad and told him what happened to me and that an ambulance was on the way. He also called my fiancé Dave and my daughter - who I had left 10 minutes earlier.

More people gathered around the two men who hovered over me. One man was an off-duty nurse. A woman in scrubs came but she never stated her occupation. She could have been a dental hygienist for all I knew. Everyone talked at once but had the same goal: to assist the woman in the car accident. I didn't know any of their names, but I will be forever grateful that they helped me.

They waited with me until the ambulance arrived 10 minutes later, making sure I was comfortable and that I didn't go into shock. I later learned that the broken granite had blocked the streets for 100 feet so the ambulance took a detour.

When the ambulance came, a man and a woman in navy blue EMT uniforms deftly snapped a rigid plastic collar around my neck. When they rolled me onto a gurney, my insides marred in agony. Obviously, something was wrong, but what?

They wheeled me away from the scene, away from my mangled car.

Had I left at my regular time of 7:15, I might not have been in the accident at all.

Had I not watched the granite falling from the truck, it might have hit me head-on.

Had I been in a smaller car, I might not have been protected so well by my SUV.

Inches and seconds saved my life.

Chapter 2

Triage

In the back of the ambulance, the male EMT jabbed my arm with a needle full of saline to keep me hydrated and some kind of medication to alleviate my aching body. The female EMT took my vitals and asked me questions.

"Do you know your name?" she asked me.

"Mary Walsh," I answered. I realized I was incredibly calm for just being in a major car accident.

"And your date of birth?"

"May 9th," I replied. Her elementary questions annoyed me but I understood why she asked them. She wanted to make sure I didn't have any head trauma.

"Do you know what happened to you?" she asked me as she filled out answers on an iPad.

"I was in a car accident," I told her the details. As the ambulance hit a bump, I shrieked out in pain.

"Where does it hurt?" She bent over me, steadying herself in the moving vehicle.

"My back," I stated. "It hurts. But I'm sure it's nothing."

She smiled at my ill attempt to downplay the situation. I didn't think anything was seriously wrong, but she probably knew better. And didn't want to tell me.

I winced trying to get comfortable on the gurney. A jolt of pain surged up my legs and into my back.

"Can I ask you to do something for me?" I asked the female EMT. "I feel so stupid asking you this because you have so many other things to take care of."

"Sure, what is it?" She dropped her iPad to the side and focused on me.

"Can you take my shoes off?" I requested. "The added two inches of my heels are making my back hurt."

She chuckled and obliged, putting my shoes in a plastic tub next to me. I found instant relief. Until the next bump in the road.

Twenty minutes later, we arrived at the emergency room of the nearest hospital. The usual ten-minute trip took twice as long because the broken granite from the accident scene blocked the roads and local traffic was rerouted causing a major backlog. I was sure other commuters were cursing at the unexpected delays.

Inside the hospital, a barrage of nurses and doctors took over. Four of them delicately moved me from the ambulance gurney to a hospital gurney. Under normal circumstances, four people didn't need to lift my 125-pound frame but they applied all caution, still unsure of my injuries. I cried out in agony as they moved me.

They rushed me into an ER room, taking more vitals, and asking additional questions about my accident.

"We need to put you into a gown," a nurse instructed me. "But I don't want to shift you too much."

Knowing exactly what she meant, I wondered out loud, "You have to cut my clothes?"

"Yes," she said, pulling scissors out of a side cabinet in the room.

She followed my silent gaze as I stared down at my brand new skirt in its maiden voyage.

"Is something wrong?" she asked, scissors steady in her hand.

I sighed. "I bought this skirt two weeks ago and it's the first time I'm wearing it." Shame on me for being worried about my clothes while I was in the middle of a bustling ER. My sacrifice was minuscule in the grand scheme of things. I sighed in defeat. "Do what you have to do."

The nurse chuckled, probably empathizing with my love for clothes and shoes. "Let me see what I can do." She laid the scissors on the counter.

"The top is old, so I don't care too much about it," I told her, "but see if you can save the skirt."

"I will try my best."

As I lay, she reached around my waist and delicately tugged on my skirt so as not to disrupt my back. The elastic waistband was a godsend; the nurse was able to gently pull the skirt over my butt and hips without causing me any additional pain. A skirt seemed like a trivial thing to worry about. Yet at that moment, it mattered to me.

After she removed my skirt, she reached for my top. Removing my shirt took a little more calculation because she had to adjust the bed upright to support my back while undressing me. She successfully lifted my top over the neck collar and kept it intact.

After the nurse tied a way-too-big gown around me, an ER doctor approached me and said, "Let's take a look at your neck." He cautiously removed the collar from around my neck. "Do you think you can move it?"

"Yes." I slowly rotated my head from side to side as he delicately poked his fingers into my neck searching for injuries.

"Wow!" he exclaimed. "You are lucky that you don't have any neck injuries. Were you wearing a seatbelt?"

"Yes," I said. "I always do."

He then pressed into my shoulders and reached underneath me as carefully as he could. "I will order an MRI and a CT scan."

"Doc," I said, raising my left arm. "I think something is wrong with my hand. It tingles and it hurts when I do this." I flexed my fingers into a fist.

He took my palm in his, examining it for any visible injuries.

"I don't see any bruising or obvious fractures," he replied. "But we'll order an x-ray anyway."

He left me and I felt like I finally had a moment to breathe. What time was it anyway? I laid still on the gurney, trying to relax as much as possible through the buzz of the ER sounds around me. Doctors and nurses clad in sea-green scrubs scuttled around the floor tending to other patients. Machines beeped and intercoms spoke news about other patients.

A few minutes later, my mom, dad, and Dave rushed into the room, hovering over my gurney. They hugged me as delicately as they could. At this point, an hour had passed since I arrived at the hospital.

"Oh my god! Oh my god!" my mom shrieked. "Are you okay? We rushed over here when we got the phone call."

"I'm fine," I reassured them. "I'm not bleeding anywhere."

Dave grabbed my left hand, running his fingers along the engagement ring he gave me six weeks earlier. Two days earlier, I put the deposit down on our reception venue and we applied for our marriage license. We had plans to get married on November 17th. Depending on how my recovery panned out would determine the fate of our wedding date.

"I love you," he told me while rubbing his flushed cheek. "I was so worried about you. The guy on the phone told me you were in a car accident but didn't say how you were. I didn't know if you were alive or dead."

He kissed me.

"Did you talk to Anita?" I asked them. In all the rush, I was unsure who told the details of the accident to my daughter.

"Yes," my mom said. "She's shaken up but I told her you were at the hospital and we'd text her when we knew more. She's on her way to school."

"Okay, thanks," I said. "The EMTs put a collar around my neck and the ER doctor was just in here and he was shocked that I didn't have any neck injury." I sighed a pause, nervous about what could be wrong with me. "He's ordering a CT and MRI for me."

My dad kissed me on the forehead. "You'll be okay," he said. "You're a fighter."

I smiled at his optimism but was still nervous about what lay ahead.

An ER nurse came into the room, interrupting us. "We will take you to get the MRI and CT scan now." My parents and Dave shuffled out of her way as the nurse took the helm of my gurney and wheeled me down the hall. "By the way," she told me, "your car accident was on the morning news. I saw it on the nurses' station TV. You're famous."

It hurt to laugh.

A few moments later, five more doctors and nurses joined her in the vestibule of the MRI room. Two of them settled to my left, two more on my right, and the last one readied himself at my feet.

"On my count, we will lift her," the ER nurse directed the others as they carefully burrowed their hands under me. I felt like I was playing that party game we used to play as kids called Light as a Feather where my friends tried to lift me from the floor. "One. Two. Three," she instructed. A second later, all six of them lifted me from the ER gurney and skillfully rested me on the MRI table. I cried out in pain again. Something throbbed in my back like I had gone fifteen rounds with Rocky Balboa.

"Are you trying to kill me?" I half-joked through an agonizing whisper. Every time someone moved me, the pain surged through me. The initial medication they gave me wasn't enough. Everything hurt. Every damn part of my body. I had never experienced so much pain in my life. Not even when both of my children were born.

That reminded me... Did someone call my son Adam at college?

"Lie as still as you can," the ER nurse instructed me. "We'll do this as quickly as possible. We can do the CT scan at the same time." The MRI table automatically moved me into the tunnel. I closed my eyes, trying to rest, as the machine buzzed around me.

Twenty minutes later, the half dozen doctors and nurses pushed an empty hospital bed into the MRI room.

"We'll move you one more time," the ER nurse told me. "I'm pretty sure this will be the last time."

I groaned and steadied myself for the onslaught of pain throughout my body as they rolled me like a log onto the bed. Because they rolled me and not lifted me, the pain was bearable. I didn't silently curse them this time.

The ER nurse pushed my bed down the hall, back to the ER room where my mom waited by herself.

"Dave left," she told me. "He had to meet a client."

"Where's Dad?" I asked her.

"He's getting us something to eat," she told me. "We never had breakfast this morning."

"There's a granola bar in my bag. Take that," I instructed her. "How's your blood sugar?" My mom headed to my bag for the granola. She needed to keep her sugar in check.

"Did anyone call Adam?" I asked her.

"Yes, Dave did before he left," my mom replied.

"Okay good," I said. "I'll call him later." Adam was a sophomore at Penn State University, two hours away.

My mom munched on the granola bar and a new doctor came into the room.

"I'm Dr. Bollinger," he said, extending his hand to me. He was young, probably 40 at best. He had an air of mature confidence about him, despite his youthful looks. "I'm a neurosurgeon here. I looked at your MRI and CT scans." As he spoke, I looked to my mom for unspoken support. "Your back is fractured. The L3 vertebrae to be exact. It's a Chance fracture. Your spine is shattered."

I didn't know exactly what the L3 vertebrae was but I knew enough that any back injury could be grave. I could be paralyzed. Shaky thoughts ran through my mind.

For the first time, tears filled my eyes.

Would I be confined to a wheelchair for the rest of my life? Would I walk again? Would I still be able to work? Would I still be able to do everything I had been actively doing all my life?

I was an independent woman who owned her own home and did everything herself. The only time I asked for help was when I couldn't reach something on a high shelf because I'm only 5'3" - and that was only if I didn't have a step stool.

And how on earth did I hoist myself from the driver's side of my car to the passenger's side with a broken back? My adrenaline must have masked the initial pain.

"It'll be okay," she said. My mom grabbed my left hand to console me. "You can do this."

"Ow." I winced. "My hand hurts when you do that."

Dr. Bollinger interrupted us, "I'll have the orthopedic surgeon come in right away and take a look at your hand. But as for your back, you have two options."

My mom and I studied him expectantly.

"One," he began, "you have surgery to fix your broken vertebrae."

I gulped in a pocket of air.

Dr. Bollinger must have taken notice of my trepidation and took a step closer to me. "It's minimally invasive surgery, but it's still surgery. I'll go in there, put rods and pins in your back to align it properly, and you'll be good as new."

"But there are risks?" my mom interjected.

"Yes," the doctor replied. "Surgery always comes with risks. Nerve damage, paralysis, infection..."

I exchanged worried glances with my mom. Paralysis? Would I be worse off than I am now?

"And my second option?" I begged the obvious question.

"You let the vertebrae heal on its own," Dr. Bollinger explained. "The recovery time is a lot longer. We're talking months versus weeks. And you run the risk of it not healing correctly on its own and you may have to have surgery down the road anyway."

I puffed out a nervous sigh. I had no idea what my best option was. Do I chance the risks of the surgery or do I let it heal on its own with no idea what could happen down the road?

"What do you recommend, Doc?"

"It's ultimately up to you. However, if it was me or my family member, I would have the surgery." He disregarded any ounce of diplomacy. "I wouldn't risk the back healing on its own. But that's me."

I was still unsure of what to do. Both options had their own set of risks.

"Tell you what," he told me. "I'll schedule the surgery for 8:00 tomorrow morning, that way it's on the books and ready to go. You can think it over today. If you decide you don't want to do it, we'll cancel it."

"Okay," was all I could muster.

"In the meantime," he pointed to my hospital bed. "You need to lie in this bed as still as you can. We don't want you to damage your back any further. The nurse will put in a catheter so you won't need to get up."

I groaned at the thought of her shoving a cold tube up my you-know-what.

"I'll have the evening nurse talk to you tonight and you can give her your decision then," he said to me. "Hopefully I'll see you in the morning."

Dr. Bollinger gave us a quick nod, turned, and left the hospital room.

"What do you think?" my mom asked me. "Whatever you decide."

"I don't know... it's too much. I can't even..."

"I know, darling."

My mom glanced at her watch. "It's almost eleven."

"Is Dad coming back soon?" I asked her.

"I hope so," she said.

A blonde woman in a white doctor coat pushed a small cart into the room, interrupting us. On her cart sat a small white metal box with a large black handle on top. A few knobs and buttons protruded from the top of it.

"Hi, I'm Dr. Bogdan," she spoke. "I'm here to check out your hand."

She gingerly lifted my left hand from the bed and placed it on a flat blank space on her cart. After removing my engagement ring and handing it to my mom, Dr. Bogdan pressed my left hand flat and splayed my fingers wide.

I winced in pain.

"This is a portable x-ray machine and it will tell us if you have a fracture," she said while lifting the metal box over my hand. She pressed a button and it made a sound like an old-school camera clicking.

"You were right when you talked to the ER doctor," she told me as she examined the x-ray. "You have a hairline fracture along your pinky into your palm. I'll have the nurse come in and wrap your hand in a soft cast."

"Thanks, Doc," I said.

With that, Dr. Bogdan packed up her machine and escaped into the humming hospital hall.

Chapter 3

Decision Time

A few hours later, Dave walked into my hospital room. A frown formed on his face when he saw me lying in my bed. He bent over the bed rail and kissed me. I had been moved to an Intensive Care room. Everything was white. The walls, the floor, the bed. Several tubes sprung out of the crease in my elbow connecting me to a heart monitor a few feet away.

"You really scared me," he told me. His normally calm features were replaced with worried eyes and pursed lips.

"I didn't mean to. Look, I broke my hand." I held up my left hand, wrapped in a splint from my palm to my elbow. Good thing I was right-handed. A broken hand was a hiccup in the grand scheme of things, but an aggravation nonetheless. "I must've gripped the steering wheel so tight that I fractured it."

"You'll be okay, baby," he told me.

"Dr. Bollinger came in earlier and said I broke my back," I said. My mouth curved downward.

"I know," Dave replied. "Your mom told me when I called her earlier."

"He recommends I have the surgery."

"I think that's a good idea," Dave concurred.

"But what if it paralyzes me?" I spoke the obvious. "What if I can't walk again? What if..."

"Then I'll push you around in a wheelchair," my fiancé reassured me. He could make me feel better in the worst situation. "We'll get through it, no matter what."

"What do you think I should do?" I asked him.

"Dr. Bollinger knows what he's doing," Dave said. "I made some calls about him and he's top-notch."

"Okay," I said. "That helps." I looked off across the stark hospital room, not concentrating on anything. "But I'm still scared."

"I know," Dave replied and kissed my forehead. "You're strong. You will get through this no matter what happens. That's part of the reason why I want to marry you."

I smiled at him for trying to cheer me up.

"Plus, you're hot," he said. "Even in that hospital gown."

I laughed out loud. Oh, it hurt to laugh.

"I should probably call Adam," I said, changing the subject. "Can you get me my phone?"

Dave reached in my purse that was sitting on a nearby wheeled table and handed me my phone.

I pulled my son's contact info up on my phone and hit Dial.

He picked up on the first ring.

"Hi," I said.

"Hi, Mom," he replied. I could instantly hear the panic in my son's voice. Even though Dave spoke to him earlier and gave him the details, Adam was still concerned.

"I'm gonna be okay," I told him. "I broke my back, and my hand, but I'm gonna be okay."

"Okay, good." Adam didn't say much, but I could tell from his quiet demeanor that he was relieved. I could have been hurt a lot worse, considering the circumstances.

"The doctor wants me to have the surgery tomorrow morning," I told him. "I'll probably do it, I just want to be sure."

"Okay, Mom," he replied. "Just call me when you can. If I can't pick up because I'm in class, I'll call you back as soon as I can."

My son was two hours away and I hated that he couldn't come to the hospital to see me. I still had to wait a few more hours to see my daughter when she was done with school for the day. I wanted to squeeze both of them so tight until their stuffing came out.

"Alright," I said to Adam. "I'll talk to you later. I love you."

"Love you too, Mom."

After I hung up the phone with Adam, I exhaled and tried to calm my nerves. All this was taking a toll on my mind and body. As a single mom for the past 10 years, I was still worried. I taught them how to cook for themselves, make their own decisions, lead by example, and to be independent and kind. I was proud of the young adults they had become. What if I couldn't teach them anymore?

What if I needed them to help me get dressed? To drive me around? To forego what they wanted to do to help me? I couldn't let that happen. I couldn't be a burden to them.

The car accident left me inches and seconds away from dying and leaving them. I still had so many things I wanted to teach them. I wanted to see them grow up into amazing adults and have families of their own. Even though their father was still in their lives, many people told me how great I raised them. That always made me smile with pride. Knowing that I was doing a good job raising my kids.

I couldn't be more proud of my kids.

"I want to have the surgery," I told Dave. I needed to be there for my kids, to be there in the fullest capacity. A small risk of paralysis outweighed permanent damage.

"Good," Dave said. "Let's tell Dr. Bollinger."

* * *

Later that afternoon, Anita walked into my hospital room. She ran up to my bed, laid next to me, and squeezed me as gently as she could. She hadn't seen me since I left her that morning and kissed her goodbye.

"Mom, some guy called me this morning and told me about your car accident. I thought you were dead." Anita's long, brown wavy hair was pulled into a knot on top of her head. She wore ripped jeans, a white short-sleeved t-shirt, and black Chuck Taylors. She was a High Honors student who spent her time playing field hockey and basketball. In her spare time, she volunteered with the special needs kids taking them to movies and bowling trips. We had yet to go on a college road trip to look at potential schools.

"What?" I exclaimed. "No, sweetie, I'm here. I'm gonna be okay." I hugged her tightly.

"All he said was 'Your mother's been in a car accident and you need to call your grandparents'. He hung up and didn't tell me how you were." She cried into my shoulder. "I didn't know if you were alive or dead."

"I'm not going anywhere," I reassured her.

"You're never allowed to leave five minutes early ever again!" She wagged a finger at me. I loved her take-no-prisoners attitude. At sixteen, she stood about 5'2" and barely weighed a hundred pounds. I often joked that she was a bulldog in the body of a chihuahua.

Anita pulled her phone out of her pocket and raised it in front of us to take a selfie. My hair was a tangled mess and I wore an ill-fitting hospital gown, but I didn't care. I was alive and with my baby girl and that's all that mattered.

Chapter 4

Surgery

Overnight, the ICU nurse on duty stuffed extra bed pillows tight between the mattress and the bed rail so that I couldn't roll around during the night. She piled pillows under my knees to alleviate pressure on my back. Slightest movements made my back feel like a dead tree about to crack open in a storm.

The staff charged me up with pain medication, but it barely relieved the pain. I was miserable. The bed button only allowed me to dispense medication every two hours so that I wouldn't get addicted. Every ounce of extra precaution was taken so that I wouldn't move and further injure my back. I lay face up all night because I wasn't allowed to lie on my side. I'd doze off, but not for long because I wanted to get comfortable and couldn't.

Let me tell you... the whole night sucked.

My body was broken and I couldn't do a damn thing about it.

Every time I moved the slightest inch, pain surged through me. Up to my shoulders and down to my toes. Show me someone who doesn't move when they sleep and I'll show you a vampire. I couldn't adjust the blankets over me without wincing in pain. I couldn't get comfortable. The nurses came in every few hours to check on me. I couldn't sleep. I was miserable.

At 7:00 on Friday morning, Dr. Bollinger met me in my room with his broadest smile.

"Are you ready?" he asked me.

"As much as I'm gonna be, Doc," I told him. I had already signed the paperwork for the surgery, so there was no turning back. I was nervous but realized surgery was my best option.

Dave and my parents hustled into my room a few moments later.

"We're here for you," my mom said. "We love you."

"You're gonna do great," Dave reassured me. He stepped over to the side of my bed and took my hand in his. My good hand.

As much as they tried to soothe my anxiety, my heart rate jumped into overdrive. Fear of never being able to walk again consumed me. My stomach grumbled in response, but probably because I hadn't eaten any solid food in 24 hours.

I had to trust Dr. Bollinger. He was my only hope.

The ICU nurse took the helm of my hospital bed and gingerly released the brakes so as not to shuffle me as she wheeled me out of the room.

She pushed me down the hall, to the operating room. We passed a few open patient rooms, each a murmur. A few other doctors walked by me, wishing me luck. A few moments later, we arrived at the operating room where Dr. Bollinger's team waited for me. Immediately, they connected me to the room's machines.

The last thing I remembered was the anesthesiologist instructing me to count backward from ten as she put a mask over my face. I think I made it to seven.

The next thing I heard were voices talking about me, but I couldn't open my eyes to see who was speaking. I think I made out my mom talking to a nurse. My hearing was intact, but why couldn't I see anything? I batted my eyes a few times to open but to no avail.

"I think she's coming around," I heard someone say.

Then I felt a hand grasp mine and I squeezed in return.

My eyes finally opened and Dave was holding my right hand. He lovingly pushed a few strands of my hair out of my face. I felt blankets on my body, but couldn't move much.

"You did great," he said. "Dr. Bollinger said everything went perfect."

"My back is fixed?" I asked him with trepidation.

"Yes," Dave replied. "You have rods and pins in your back, but you're almost as good as new. Dr. Bollinger will be in in a little while to tell you more details. He wanted to see you before he left for the day."

"Those rods and pins are inside me for the rest of my life?" I wanted to know.

"Yes," Dave answered.

A couple of nurses enclosed on my bed. My mom and dad followed them.

"How are you feeling?" one asked me. The other one checked my vitals and lifted the blanket to expose my toes.

"Okay, I guess," I replied. While straining to watch the second nurse without shifting my body, I watched as the second nurse ran a pen along the bottom of my feet.

"Can you feel that?" she asked me.

"Yes," I replied, almost annoyed that she asked me an obvious question. Why wouldn't I? But then I realized that she was checking to make sure I avoided paralysis. I couldn't move, but I could feel her pen jabbing into my foot. That was a good sign.

"Can I get you anything?" she offered.

"I'm starving," I growled.

"You need to be on a liquid diet for the next 24 to 48 hours, but I'll see if I can get you some chicken broth." She left us and walked out of the room.

"You're gonna be fine." My mom leaned over me. "I talked to your boss and she sends her well wishes. She had plans to tell everyone at your work how you were doing."

"Thank you," I said. "I sent some texts out yesterday, but not to--"

"What's wrong?" the nurse asked me, probably noticing I didn't finish my sentence.

"I'm gonna be sick," I blurted, stretching my neck forward. After-effects from the anesthesia.

The nurse quickly grabbed a small plastic bag that surrounded a circular wire and handed it to me.

Just in time. But, oh, did my back ache from puking. I groaned in response.

"If you can warn me the next time," she told me, "I'll hold your back steady so you don't strain it. You'll need to keep it still. It's fragile because your spine needs to heal. I know it will hurt."

"You probably won't want to eat that chicken broth now," Dave jested. Gently, he patted a cool cloth on my forehead and wiped my face.

"Thank you," I told him, exhausted from expelling every last ounce out of my body.

"Now that you're awake, I will head into the office," Dave told me. "Your mom and dad will stay with you and I'll come back after work. And Anita will come visit you after school."

I puked two more times in the next hour. The nurses attempted to alleviate the agony I felt but to no avail. Even though misery wove its way through me, my spine avoided further injury.

Finally, after an evil laugh, my stomach stopped torturing me.

Chapter 5

Visitors

On Saturday, many of my friends came to visit me. Even though I was high on pain medication, I hoped I maintained intelligible conversations with them. I could always blame my zoning out on the potent drugs. They brought flowers, balloons, and get-well cards. I couldn't ask for better friends.

Many more sent texts or called saying they would come to visit as soon as they had the chance. All of them were astonished, and thankful, that I survived a freak accident. No one cried, which helped me stay upbeat. Even though we all knew it, no one wanted to admit that I was inches away from dying.

Visiting with everyone exhausted me because I wanted to rest, but I didn't let on. I wanted to talk with each of them, to soothe their worries that I would be fine.

Then Kristin, one of my best friends, came to visit. As soon as she hugged me in my bed, tears filled her eyes.

"It's okay," I reassured her as she released me. "I'm not going anywhere."

"I can't help it," she said. "I almost lost you. You could have died." Kristin spoke the elephant in the room and what no one else stated before, maybe because my other friends were too afraid to admit the horror of my circumstances.

While Kristin visited me, my parents came into the room. They had plans to go to Pittsburgh for the weekend but canceled their plans to stay with me.

"My surgery went well and I'll be in the hospital for a few more days. You should still head to Pittsburgh. Where am I gonna go?" I said, motioning to the cords tethering me to a saline pouch and a heart monitor.

"No," my mom said. "We'll stay here and take care of things at your house." My mom had already done a few loads of my laundry and tossed some leftovers on the verge of growing mold out of my fridge. I was thankful for the extra help.

My dad brought my laptop because the hospital TV channels lacked compared to my selection at home. No Netflix. No DVR. No On Demand. I needed to be connected to the outside world. I attempted to read a book, but the drugs made me tired and I often dozed off after the second page.

Later that afternoon, Dave came to see me, escorting another man. I didn't recognize the guy because I was high on pain medication. The man had a mostly full head of dark hair, sprinkled with some salt and pepper on the sides. He stood a few inches taller than Dave.

"Babe," Dave said, "this is Scott. He's an attorney who will take your case. My company is familiar with his firm."

Whoa. I remembered Dave saying something the day before about hiring an attorney, but exhaustion and drugs blurred my memory of the details. Dave had also called my medical and auto insurance companies. He was a godsend to take care of everything and let me heal. I needed to marry him. Oh wait, I was.

Of course, there would be a lawsuit. Someone's negligence nearly killed me. Was the driver speeding through the S-curve? Was the truck overloaded? Were the strappings worn out? Someone was responsible for my near-death injuries.

I never thought suing someone would come to fruition so quickly. Maybe certain attorneys are called "ambulance chasers" for a reason? My surgery was only 24 hours earlier. I lay in the ICU strapped to monitors, barely able to move. I couldn't even get up and go to the bathroom. The previous 48 hours completely changed my life. Now I was stuck in a bed feeling isolated and frustrated. I had more important things on my mind at the moment than a lawsuit.

Good thing Dave was there because I couldn't concentrate on what Scott was saying. I think he asked me some questions about the accident and what I remembered. He handed me a folder of documents to read over and sign as soon as possible.

I had never been involved in a lawsuit before. That wasn't the kind of person I was. If I spilled hot coffee on myself after going through a fast-food drive-thru, that was my fault, not the corporation who didn't warn me that coffee was hot. Duh, coffee is hot.

However, my back was also broken, and Dr. Bollinger told me that I needed to wear a back brace for six to twelve weeks. During that time, I wouldn't be able to drive (not that I had any desire to yet), bend down to tie my shoes, or carry a laundry basket. I wouldn't be able to do the things I was used to doing on my own. A babysitter was in my near future.

I needed to sign the litigation documents if I wanted any kind of due process.

"I talked to the police," Scott explained, "and received their first draft of the police report. It turns out that truck coming at you was carrying 14 tons of granite. Once it fell off the truck, it shattered all over the road and blocked the street for a hundred yards. You were literally hit by a ton of bricks."

Dave and I exchanged nervous glances. We both knew I could have been hurt a lot worse. I didn't want to dwell on the other outcome.

Scott continued, "Along with the local authorities, the department of transportation was called, as well as the telephone company. The street was shut down for half a day while everyone cleaned it up."

"I never do anything half-ass," I joked.

"Plus, I went to the impound to check out your car," Dave added. "The entire undercarriage was sliced off. Gone. Good thing you swerved when you did."

Holy hell.

Had I been hit head-on, I might have lost my legs. Or worse.

* * *

All of the doctors and nurses that I met during my stay were amazing. Each one was courteous, professional, and personable. They made me feel at ease by being calm and stating my progress, despite my dire situation. Later that evening, the ICU nurse came into my room to check my temperature and blood pressure. He was no different than his predecessors.

"How are you feeling tonight?" he asked me, reviewing my heart monitor. "All of your numbers look good. What's your pain level?"

"About a seven, but I feel pretty good," I told him. "But I'm hungry. Am I allowed to have anything yet? I haven't eaten anything in over two days."

After my puking episode the previous day, Dr. Bollinger restricted me to water and pumped fluids. My stomach gurgled from the vacancy.

"Yes," the ICU nurse said. "I read your chart and you can have something now, but only a liquid diet. Your choices are chicken broth or chicken broth."

I laughed at his feeble attempt to cheer me up.

"I guess I'll take chicken broth," I said.

"Good choice," he said. "I'll be right back with it."

He returned a few minutes later with a small Styrofoam container and a plastic spoon in his hands. After he put the items on the rolling tray next to my bed, he lifted the lid to a small puff of steam. He pulled another small container full of a red substance from his pocket and set it on my tray.

"I brought you some Jell-O too," he told me. "I hope you like strawberry."

"Thank you." I offered him a grateful smile. Jell-O wasn't tiramisu, but I was thankful for something other than water and chicken broth.

"Let me help you sit up a little bit," he said. "You're not allowed to lean over your bed."

As he hit the button to raise the top of my bed, I let out a scream. Pain surged through me. Every damn nerve. Would it ever lessen?

"I'm so sorry," he apologized profusely. "I forgot to warn you when I move your bed."

"It's okay," I sputtered through gritted teeth. The slightest movement made me feel like ten thousand hand grenades exploded inside me.

"I know it will be hard to sleep tonight," he assured me, "but I'll tuck some extra pillows next to you to limit your movement."

"Thank you," I said. "I appreciate everything you all do for me." I pulled the wheeled tray closer to my bed to eat the chicken broth and Jell-O. He may have brought the food to my room, but he didn't need to push the tray to me. I was fully capable.

I took a spoonful and almost immediately gagged. "I know hospital food is supposed to be bad and I haven't eaten anything in two days, but this is gross."

The ICU nurse laughed out loud.

Chapter 6

They tried to make me go to rehab but I said no, no, no...

After three days in the ICU, I spent two more days in a regular hospital room where I wasn't tethered to as many machines constantly checking my heart rate and oxygen levels. Nor did I have a blood pressure cuff pumping my arm every half hour.

More friends and family came to visit me when they could. Vases full of flowers and balloons filled my room. The fresh aroma of carnations and daisies made me happy despite being in a sterile hospital room.

As the days progressed, I eased my way into a solid diet without puking. Hospital food lacked flavor, but at least I could keep it down. Baby steps.

Dr. Bollinger gave me a *nice* back brace to wear from my neck to my waist. It Velcroed snugly around my hospital gown. The fashion gods would never approve. The only time I could remove it was when I slept flat on my back or when I took a shower. Dr. Bollinger told me I had to wear it every day for the next six to twelve weeks. Admittedly, I am an overachiever, so I planned to be out of it by week six.

My catheter was removed, too. Because of the extent of my injury, the nurses were required to assist me to the bathroom to prevent me from falling. I tried to tell them I would be fine on my own, but they weren't buying what I was selling. I wasn't allowed to bend or twist my back, but I was leaps and bounds ahead of what I felt five days earlier. However, I didn't expect that squatting down would be so hard. I gritted my teeth through the pain. Who knew you bent your back at the same time? Thankfully the bathroom had handrails.

I was determined to do everything myself. Before all this, I cut my grass and shoveled my snow (except when I made Adam do it). One summer, I built my garden bed from scratch, hauling 4x4 railroad ties from Home Depot, drilling holes, and pounding heavy-duty one-inch spikes into them. Nobody helped me. Nor did I want any help. I supported myself for years and I wouldn't stop now.

On the morning of Day Five, my nurse walked into my room holding a couple of papers. She was my new best friend. After all, she came into the bathroom with me and helped me go. (Isn't that what a best friend did?)

"These are your discharge and physical therapy forms." She handed them to me to read and sign.

"I'm going home today?" I perked up. I couldn't wait to go home. I missed my dog Charlotte. I missed my bed. I missed my lumpy couch.

"No," she said. "You're being transferred to a rehab hospital. You'll get physical therapy there."

My proverbial balloon buzzed around the room as the air blurted out of it in quick cadence.

"A rehab hospital?" I balked. "No, I want to go home."

"Do you have stairs in your house?" she asked.

"Yes."

"And your bedroom is on the second floor?"

"Yes."

"Then you're not going home," she replied. "There is no way you will walk up those steps by yourself. Not in your condition. You can barely make it ten feet to the bathroom." I appreciated her bluntness, but she didn't know how strong I was. Or how determined I wanted to do everything for myself.

"What if I stay at Dave's house?" I countered. Dave had a bedroom and a full bathroom on his first floor.

"Will he be home with you all day for the next week to take care of you?" she asked me.

"No," I moaned. "He has to go to work."

"Well, then it looks like you're heading to rehab," the nurse chuckled.

"How long do I have to stay there?" I groaned.

"At least a week."

I rolled my eyes. She won. This time.

A couple of hours later, two men wearing EMT uniforms pushed an empty gurney into my room and stopped it adjacent to my bed. Oh no, not again.

"We will move you onto this gurney," the taller one said. "Just relax and we'll roll you onto it." Easier said than done.

I held my breath as they lowered the rails on my bed and gingerly rolled me onto the gurney. Despite their best efforts, I squealed in pain. No wonder everyone was so nice to me. They were secretly trying to torture me.

The men wheeled me down the hall, into the elevator, and into the ambulance bay, not always avoiding hiccups on the floor. An empty ambulance waited for me, back doors welcoming me in. I felt like I was piloting my starfighter into the belly of a mothership.

Twenty minutes later, my ambulance arrived at the rehab hospital.

Chapter 7

Going Vertical

The EMTs registered me at the front desk of the rehab hospital, handed me over, and quickly departed. The rehab hospital differed from a regular hospital by not having an emergency room nor doctors and nurses scuttling frantically around the halls.

A middle-aged woman stood from behind the desk and took over where the EMTs left off. As she pushed me down the hall to my new room, I glanced into other patient rooms as I passed them. One man sat in a wheelchair talking to his visitors. Another hobbled with a walker. A woman lay on a bed snuggled in blankets. Another woman passed me in the hall in a wheelchair, her physical therapist pushing her. All of them, I guessed, were at least 30 years older than me.

"We're here," the woman pushing my gurney said with a broad smile. "This will be your new home for a little while."

I gulped down a breath. I didn't want to be there, but accepted my fate and smiled at her attempt to make me feel welcome.

The woman from the front desk pointed to the other side of the room, to an elderly woman lying in a bed. "This is Dorothy," she told me. "Your roommate."

"Hi, Dorothy," I called to her, and received a whispered "Hi" in return.

The woman aligned my gurney next to my bed. "Let's get you into your bed," she said. "But you'll have to learn to do this yourself, so I'll only give you minimal assistance." She took a defensive stance next to me like a linebacker, her arms stretched out ready to catch me if I fell.

Through gritted teeth, I slowly rolled myself on my right side, biting down the pain. I put a hand next to my waist and gingerly raised my upper body. Since my left hand was broken, I put all of my weight on my right. What seemed like an hour later, but was probably only 20 seconds, I sat upright on the gurney. I didn't want to move in any direction for fear of having pain surge through me again.

"Now what?" I asked the woman, eyeing the logistics of getting me from the gurney to the bed. My legs filled in the gap between the gurney and my new bed. I sat as still as I could.

"Like this," she said.

The woman grabbed my back brace that had been lying at the foot of my gurney and wrapped it around my waist. She held a locked elbow out to me as I grabbed onto it and hoisted myself into a standing position. She helped me slowly rotate my body 180 degrees. We performed the same steps in reverse so that I could lay on the bed. Everyday procedures that I never thought twice about now needed a plan of attack.

Moments later, a dark-haired woman in a navy blue golf shirt came into the room and approached me.

"I'm Christina." She offered me her hand. "I'm one of your main physical therapists. I'll keep track of your progress while you're here. You'll meet John when you go into the PT gym later." She wrote her and his name on the whiteboard on the wall across from my bed. Then she wrote my physical therapy session times on the calendar grid. "You're scheduled for PT twice a day along with OT for your broken hand."

"Okay!" I was excited to do something besides sit in my bed all day. Watching TV and reading were getting old. I even tried to put on the appearance that I wasn't a patient confined to a bed. My mom had brought me some regular clothes to wear in the morning. Even though I didn't normally wear t-shirts and yoga pants, they were red-carpet worthy above oversized unisex vented hospital gowns.

"I'll let you get some lunch," Christina said, "then I'll come back for you in about an hour and we'll see what you can do."

After my lunch of bland chicken salad with a side of bread and butter, Christina returned pushing an empty wheelchair.

"Are you ready?" she asked.

"Yes."

Even though my brain grasped the concept of the actions that I needed to take to get into the wheelchair, my body didn't want to cooperate. I rolled onto my right side and pushed my weight up. But then I fell back onto the mattress because I didn't put my elbow at the best angle and I lost my balance. Ugh.

"Let's try this again," I laughed at myself. I adjusted my right elbow to a better angle and pushed myself upward into a sitting position. Christina waited patiently while I did it all myself.

"That's great!" she said to me as she helped me into the wheelchair. "You did that without any help. What's your pain level?"

"About a five-six," I told her. The pain wasn't as bad as it was in the regular hospital but stuck around to remind me that it was there. The worst I had was a nine in the other hospital, because a ten would have been near death for me and, luckily, that hadn't happened.

Christina pushed my wheelchair down the hallway toward the physical therapy gym.

We entered a large room full of patients and therapists. One older man cycled reps in a stationary bike. Another gripped a three-foot-tall wooden bar to help him walk a few steps. An older woman in a chair pushed a large rubber ball in front of her back and forth with her feet. The room buzzed with encouraging conversations, clicking machines, and metal walkers being pushed along the tile floor.

A man dressed in the same color golf shirt as Christina approached us. He had dark hair and glasses.

"This is John," she said. "He and I will be in charge of your care while you're here. But I need to go see another patient." Christina left us.

"Hi," John said to me. "I heard about your car accident. A nurse showed me a picture of your car that was on the news."

"Yeah, that was me," I confirmed.

"You're so lucky," he said. "I can't even imagine…"

"Oh, yes, I know."

John continued, "Let's see what you can do here. Do you want to try to walk?"

"Yes!" For the past five days, I had either been confined to a wheelchair, a gurney, or a hospital bed. My land legs were grossly out of practice.

John grabbed a metal walker from the sidewall of the room and attached a platform to the top for my broken hand. He put it in front of my wheelchair and took a step back. Challenge accepted!

I initially reached for it with my left hand, but quickly pulled it back remembering I could not put any weight on it. Then I reached for the walker with my right hand and slowly pulled myself into a standing position. I puffed out a long breath as I stood.

"Are you okay?" John asked me.

"Yeah, just taking it all in," I told him. I hadn't been vertical in days. The view differed from up there.

"You ready to take a step?"

I nodded.

John crouched to my side ready to help me move my legs if I needed it. "Once you step, move the walker in front of you. Then repeat that pattern. Step. Move. Step. Move."

A week earlier, I never imagined that someone would teach me how to walk again.

I took a small step, then pushed the walker as far as my right arm could reach. I took another step and pushed the walker again.

"Good!" John encouraged me. "How far do you think you can go?"

"Back home," I half-joked.

"Nice try," John chuckled. "Try to go to the end of the wooden bar down there. That's a hundred feet." He pointed to a stationary weight bar that stretched out in the middle of the room.

A hundred feet? Surely I could walk that. Under normal circumstances, I could tackle a hundred feet in my sleep. He didn't know who he was talking to.

Determinedly, I took a step and moved the metal walker. I took another one. And another one. John watched me and smiled in approval. He strode next to me, without any help. Admittedly, I was a little jealous.

"Keep going," he encouraged me. "You're doing great!"

Even though it took me almost a minute, I walked the hundred feet. The back brace wrapped around me limited my stride, but I did it. I pumped my right fist into the air at the finish line.

"Good job!" John congratulated me.

At this point, my back injury was an inconvenience to me. I didn't feel sorry for myself and I wanted to push myself to get back to the way I was a week earlier. Rods and pins in my back wouldn't stop me. But my legs had other ideas and practically taunted me.

John worked with me for the next half hour testing my strength, dexterity, and balance. As instructed, I marched around the room and stepped up and down on short risers. John also made me do leg lifts and exercises similar to ballet plies. Some of the training seemed elementary to me, but I did what he told me. After all, he knew what he was doing.

*　*　*

Later that evening, I awoke with a start to Dave standing above my bed. He came to visit me every night after work.

"How long have you been here?" I asked him with groggy eyes.

"A few minutes," he said. "I let you sleep. They must've pushed you hard in rehab today."

I didn't think so earlier, but Dave was right.

Chapter 8

Meeting The Cool Kids

Over the next three days, John or Christina pushed a wheelchair into my room and rolled me down the hallway to the gym for more rounds of physical and occupational therapy. I wasn't allowed to walk anywhere on my own. Not even to the bathroom. If I attempted to go rogue, a bed alarm sounded and a desk nurse came rushing into the room. I cannot confirm or deny that I might've accidentally tested it.

At each therapy session, Christina and John pushed me to walk farther, do more reps, and stand longer on my own. And each afternoon, I took a nap. I couldn't believe how tired I was. Despite the rumors I had heard that hospitals were boring, I took all the rest I could get.

My first roommate, Dorothy, was discharged and another elderly woman occupied the vacant bed in my room. Her name was

Evelyn and she was 96. I had a tough time talking to her because she had trouble hearing. But I tried.

On the fourth day, instead of doing exercises, the physical therapists called all of us patients into a circle of chairs. Fifteen of us ditched our walkers, gritted our teeth through the pain as we squatted down, and settled into the padded chairs. As the baby of the group, my older cohorts took every opportunity to tease me about it. I had chatted with several of them during my stay and we compared injury stories. Two men had strokes. A woman was t-boned in her car and broke her leg. Another fell down her steps. We became fast friends, encouraging each other to keep pushing during our exercises. We felt each other's pain like no one else could.

A therapist named Margaret led our group. She wore the same blue golf shirt that Christina and John did.

"Hi everyone," Margaret said, moving her hands in a welcoming gesture. "I've seen some of you talking to each other during therapy sessions, but wanted to gather everyone together and chat."

We all glanced at each other wondering what Margaret wanted to do.

Margaret continued, "Today we'll go around the circle, state our name, and say what we love." She eyed her circle and didn't get any volunteers. "I'll go first... My name is Margaret. I love my family and my job and my dog." She had probably done this many times before with different audiences.

The older woman to Margaret's left was next. The woman wore black trousers, a soft red sweater, pearls around her neck, and makeup. I cringed, embarrassed that I wasn't dressed as well as her in my black yoga pants, gym t-shirt, and bare face. I was lucky that I brushed my hair that morning. My attire was quite the contrast to the dresses and heels that I wore to work and made sure my face was done.

The woman in the red sweater said, "My name is Barbara and I love my husband and my kids and grandkids."

The next few people told us that they loved their family, their pets, and their friends.

Then my turn came. Of course, I loved my kids, my family, and my fiancé. That was a given.

"My name is Mary," I choked up a little, "and I love that I met all of you." I gestured to my new friends who encircled me. "I never would have met any of you had I not been in a car accident because my regular days keep me from opportunities like this." It was true. I worked with people close to my age, my neighbors were young, and my kids were teenagers. Being around older folks was not a regular thing for me. I had a newfound respect for my new friends.

The elderly man to my left took his turn. He had told me during a previous exercise session that he had heart surgery two weeks earlier.

Everyone in the circle took their turn and prepared themselves to get up and move with their walkers. Margaret approached me as I was trying to stand into mine.

"I was impressed with what you said," she told me. "I looked around the circle as you were speaking and everyone smiled."

"Thank you," I said. "But it's true. I'm so thankful I met everyone." I teared up again. I couldn't believe I was so emotional. I was not a crier. I didn't even cry at the end of *A Star is Born*.

* * *

After a week in the rehab hospital, I was used to my new schedule of doing therapy in the morning after breakfast and again after lunch. John or Christina would write my session times on the whiteboard in my room in the morning and come and get me with a wheelchair to go down the hall. In the gym, I graduated from the metal walker and advanced to a cane. Taking strides was still slow going, but I was progressing.

One night the dining director came by and offered me soft tacos instead of the bland, standard fare. Without a second thought, I took him up on it, chowing down on the rare delicacy.

On the seventh day, my session was supposed to start in a couple of minutes and Christina was nowhere to be found. I took it upon myself to get to the gym and grabbed my cane. Slowly, I made my way down the hall toward the gym. By this time, I no longer had a bed alarm if I stood up on my own. The freedom of walking by myself for the first time in almost two weeks was liberating.

"Oh, there you are," Christiana called from behind me. She quickly caught up to me, taking faster strides than me. "I went to your room and you were gone. I'm sorry I was late. A doctor caught me in the hall and wanted to talk about another patient."

"Look, I'm walking by myself," I boasted.

"I see that. You're doing great!" she replied. "How's your pain level?"

"Not bad," I said, resting against my cane. "Like a two-three. But that's what it's been for a few days now. Not terrible but enough to let me know it's there."

Christina accompanied me the rest of the way to the gym, lessening her pace. What should take a few seconds to walk took me a couple of minutes. I struggled because I was never one to be patient.

Chapter 9

Heading Home

On the following Wednesday, John came into my room and handed my discharge papers to me. After thirteen days in two different hospitals, I was finally going home! My left wrist was bound in a splint and I had to wear a back brace for at least another month, but I couldn't wait to be back in my own place. I was lucky to be heading home after eight days in the rehab hospital. Some patients were there for months.

All of the staff I met had been amazing and they encouraged me to do more without being pushy. They never let me give up and kept a smile on their faces even when I had no interest in what they were trying to teach me. Day 13 was a short advance from Day 12, but both were leaps and bounds from Day One. When I was admitted, I couldn't pull myself from the bed without assistance and spent most days pushed around in a wheelchair. Now I was cruising the halls with a cane.

OT taught me to fold clothes in a simulated laundry room, put groceries into a shopping cart, and carry lightweight items. PT taught me to get in and out of a car without bending my back. It's not as easy as it sounds. I steadied my legs backward into a stance up against the edge of the car, then slowly lowered my core to sit on the seat. Without twisting my waist, I learned to shift my entire body as a whole to face forward in the car. I had never thought about the dynamics of getting into a car until then. Folks with bad knees have to face this struggle all the time. I instantly joined their secret society as a new recruit.

My progression was slow going and the snail pace annoyed me, but I never thought I *wouldn't* get better.

"Are you excited to go home?" John asked me.

"Yes!" I said. "But I'm heading to Dave's house for a few days first. He has a bedroom and a full bath on his first floor so I will camp out there."

"Good," John replied. "You won't have to worry about stairs yet. Your legs are strong, but we don't want you falling."

"You all have been fantastic, but I'd rather not come back here if I don't have to," I joked.

John laughed. "You will, however, have to go to outpatient physical therapy three times a week for at least the next two months. It's right next door so we know everyone over there. They're great."

"And what happens after two months? Am I done?" I wanted to know if I could reduce the number of sessions per week.

"Possibly. They'll reassess you," John explained. "You've come a long way in the past week. In two months, they'll be able to tell you when you can go back to work."

Work. I was in no shape to go back to work. I wanted to get back to my routine, but I couldn't drive and I would not confirm or deny that I enjoyed my afternoon naps to rest.

With little assistance from John, I pulled myself out of bed (my biceps were getting a great workout!) and grabbed my cane. He escorted me down the hall to the gym for my final inpatient physical therapy session.

When we entered the gym, he announced, "Hey everyone, today is Mary's last day here. She is heading home!" Other therapists and patients hooted and hollered at my success. I had befriended so many people there, I almost hated to leave. Almost.

Through bittersweet hugs, I made my way around the room to everyone. I was thankful that I was moving on and wished them well in their progression. Hopefully, all of the other patients could be home soon, too.

John then handed me some at-home exercise sheets and walked back to my room with me. Like in the hospital, my strict at-home orders included no bending, lifting, or twisting at the waist. My back brace would prevent a lot of it, but I still had to be careful.

"Is someone coming to get you?" he asked me.

"Yes," I replied. "My friend Paul. He's taking me to Dave's house." Since I was being discharged at lunchtime, Dave couldn't get out of work to take me home. Paul worked near the hospital and could easily help me. Paul and I met 10 years earlier when we used to work together and had been great friends ever since.

"Okay, good." John gathered my bag of clothes, my laptop, my medications, and the care items that were given to me, including a long-handled sponge to use in the shower. Over the previous few days, I had mastered taking a shower on my own while sitting still in a shower chair. But the hospital shower had a hand sprayer, a luxury I didn't have at home. The logistics remained to be seen.

Paul arrived in my room ten minutes later and loaded my personal items into his car. I hated that I relied on other people to carry my things, but I couldn't put any stress on my back.

With an excited fist pump, I grabbed my cane and walked down the hall to the exit doors.

The same doors I came through eight days earlier laying on a gurney from the back of an ambulance.

Chapter 10

Choose to be Grateful

When Paul pulled into Dave's driveway, he hit the lip of the pavement. His car bounced a few times, sending excruciating pain through my body.

"Ahhhhhh!" I wailed. I hadn't been in a car in almost two weeks and forgot how bumpy the lip in the driveway could be.

"I'm so, so sorry," Paul panicked, reaching out for me as a mom does to her child in the front seat when she has to slam on the brakes.

"It's okay," I reassured him. "I didn't expect that bump to be there. I'll know better next time."

Paul parked the car, exited his door, and walked around to my side to help me. Remembering my mock-car exit strategy from the rehab hospital, I grabbed onto the overhead hand bar, shifted my entire body to the right, and pulled myself to a standing position.

Every move I made had to be calculated. I could no longer jump in and out of a car or flop onto an overstuffed chair.

At the front of the two-story house, I opened the garage door with the push button code. Paul followed me into the house, carrying my things.

My dog Charlotte, a brown and white American Staffordshire Terrier, raced at me because she hadn't seen me in two weeks. Dave kept her while I was in the hospital. Charlotte jumped at me, tail wagging, excited that I was home again. Paul skirted in between us, grabbing Charlotte by the collar to prevent her from knocking me over. She settled down, thrilled that her mistress was back.

Paul settled me on the couch in the family room and put everything I needed within reach so that I didn't have to get up: my cane, a bottle of water, the TV remote, a blanket. Dave wasn't expected home for a couple more hours and Paul needed to get back to work. Charlotte settled at my feet. Ironically, I needed to get up as often as I could, even if it meant only fifteen feet into the kitchen. I couldn't sit or stand in one position for too long though.

After I spent the next few hours watching afternoon TV, Dave came home with a to-go box from Snappers, one of our favorite restaurants. Hospital food was less than desirable and I was ready to eat a real meal.

"I brought you a butternut squash and roasted beet salad with chicken," Dave said. "I know you love it."

"You're amazing," I told him. "I can't wait to marry you."

He winked at me.

Dave opened the package and put it on the kitchen table. I grabbed my cane and hobbled over to him.

I devoured that salad like I hadn't eaten in a month. It was full of flavor, unlike the staple, bland chicken breasts and fish patties at the hospital.

Later that night, Dave laid with me in bed. He had readied the first-floor guest bedroom so I wouldn't have to climb the stairs where he slept.

He brushed a strand of hair out of my eyes. Except for my neck, I couldn't move much, still fearful that I could damage my back.

"You've been such a trouper through all this," he told me.

I gazed at him. Even in the dim light of the room, I could get lost in his sapphire eyes. The same color that matched my engagement ring on my left hand. The same hand that was mostly wrapped in a cast.

He continued, "If it was me laid up in that hospital bed with those injuries, I'd be crying like a baby every day. You've been so brave and I've never heard you complain once."

"I can't complain," I told him. "I'm still here. I'm so lucky I wasn't hurt worse. After being in that hospital for a couple of weeks, I met so many other people that have it worse than me. If they aren't complaining, then I can't feel sorry for myself. Someone else is happy with less than what I have." I had the choice to be angry about what happened or thankful that I wasn't six feet underground. I chose the latter.

A small tear trickled out of my eye and down my cheek.

"Don't cry, baby," he told me, wiping the tear away. "Everything will be okay."

"It's just that..." I began, so ashamed that I showed my weakness. "Sometimes it's hard. Everything is hard. I can't do anything that I used to do. I can't even walk without using a cane. I have to rely on you and so many other people to do things for me. I hate it." More tears flowed out of my eyes. My frustration built up over the past two weeks and finally popped. I was glad that Dave was with me. He made things easier.

"It's fine," Dave reassured me. "We will do what we can for you. We are so thankful that you weren't killed. I don't know what I would have done if I had lost you."

I offered him a weak smile.

Dave continued, "When that guy called me from your phone that morning... well, first I thought, why is another man calling me from your phone... and then he told me you were in a car accident. I dropped everything and raced to the hospital."

He kissed me.

"You amaze me every day," he said.

Chapter 11

Getting Dressed was a Win

The next morning, Dave woke me up before he headed to work. I clenched the covers in my fists as I opened my eyes. I pursed my lips at him as he sat next to me on the bed.

"Are you okay?" he asked. "You look upset."

"No," I told him. "I had a terrible nightmare. Not like I was back in the car accident, but that someone was attacking me, trying to kill me."

"It's okay," Dave reassured me. "You're here. You're fine now."

"I've been having these nightmares for the past few nights," I told him. "I didn't want to say anything though. It's been terrible stuff. Knife fights. Car chases. Bombings. And now this attack."

"I think your body is reacting to the accident," Dave explained. "If they continue, I can take you to the doctor."

"Nah, I'll be fine." I didn't want to go to yet *another* doctor for something that could be temporary.

"Are you sure?"

"Yes, I'm positive," I told him.

"Okay, then I'm heading to work. Anything special you want for dinner tonight?"

"Surprise me," I told him.

Dave kissed me and headed out the door. Wow, he looked good in his suit. I developed a new crush on him every time he wore one. How's that song go... 'every girl's crazy 'bout a sharp-dressed man'? But I digress...

After Dave left, Charlotte trotted into my bedroom and stared at me.

"I sure hope Dave let you out this morning," I told her, still lying on my bed. "Otherwise you'll be doing the potty dance until I can get myself out of bed and down the hall. And that might be a while."

She didn't react to my joke. Not even a tail wag. What a tough crowd.

"Okay, let's do this," I told her, acting like she could have a conversation with me. Too bad she didn't have opposable thumbs; she might have been able to help me. I heaved a heavy sigh and slowly rolled on my side. This was the first time I attempted to get out of bed without assistance, hospital bed handrails, or an emergency nurse call button. Stupid me didn't think about having Dave help me before he left. That nurse was right when she wouldn't let me go home after the first hospital. No way could I have taken care of myself a week ago.

"Ow, ow, ow, ow..." I winced as I steadied my good hand beneath me and gingerly raised my healing torso to a sitting position. Dave had put my back brace at the foot of my bed the previous night and I reached for it.

Crap, it was too far away. I couldn't grasp it without bending my back. Now what? I looked around the room for some improvisational help. Almost everything was out of reach. In an aha moment, I pulled on the bed covers, inching the back brace toward me, trying to sit as still as possible. Patience was not my forte. With a few tugs, I grabbed it and wrapped it around my pajamas.

My cane was propped against the wall next to my bed within easy reach. Score one for me.

Dave had the good foresight to put all of my clothes in the top dresser drawers so that I wouldn't have to bend down to get them. I grabbed some underwear, a neon green t-shirt, and a black pair of leggings. With my clean clothes stuffed under the arm of my bad hand and my cane in the other, I shuffled to the bathroom to take a shower. I must've been a riotous sight!

In the bathroom, Dave had laid out shampoo, soap, a washcloth, a bag for my arm cast, a clean towel, and my long-handled sponge from the hospital. If he hadn't done this for me, I would have added an extra ten minutes to take a shower. He also made sure my shower chair was secured to the bottom of the tub and near the faucet handles. He was a godsend.

After having put my back brace on minutes earlier, I needed to take it off to get in the shower. I delicately removed the back brace, trying to keep my body as still as possible. Oh, this was slow going. Like in a chess game, I methodically planned out what my next three moves would be to do daily tasks that I never thought twice about. Taking for granted my level of reliance, this process differed from my pre-accident days because of my limited mobility.

With the back brace removed and placed within reach, I peeled off my clothes. The pajamas weren't so bad because I could lift them over my head without moving my back. But do you have any idea how hard it is to remove underwear without bending your back?

Crap. If I only had my long-handled grabber. It was still in my bedroom. I made a mental note to keep it with me at all times. I would need to sprout another arm for all the things I carried. I grunted at the newfound struggle as I found an inventive way to remove my underwear by sliding each side down bit by bit then allowing gravity to take over once they passed my hips.

Then I bagged my hand so my cast wouldn't get wet. This was the final step, otherwise, I would be even more of an invalid trying to take a shower without the use of my fingers.

Steadily, I stepped into the tub, sat in the shower chair, and turned on the water. Ahhh... I closed my eyes as the rainfall of droplets cascaded on top of me.

With my long hair, shampooing was an undertaking. How on earth would I be able to rinse all of it with one free hand *and* without bending my back? Guys with short hair had it easy. They didn't have to think about these things. I was already running up the water bill because I did everything at a snail's pace, so conditioning my hair was out of the question.

I grabbed the long-handled sponge, held it between my knees with my bagged hand, and squirted body wash on it with my good hand. What a hassle. I couldn't put myself through this every day and decided to shower every other day. It's not like I was out sweating at the gym and stinking up the place.

After I showered, I quickly toweled off and removed the bag from my bad hand to free up my fingers. I put on a shirt and my back brace. The less time without the brace, the better. The brace gave me some support and physically stopped me from bending over.

Now came the fun part: putting on some underwear.

I felt like a contortionist at the circus as I bent mostly-unused parts of my body to slide the underwear on. But going commando was not an option. If I had the long-handled grabber, I would have had an easier time. Another mental note.

I carried the leggings into the bedroom and eyed them up. As I struggled to balance myself while standing on one foot to put them on, I felt like Tom Hanks in *Big* trying to yank on too-small jeans and falling on the floor. (Gosh, I'm showing my age...)

A few minutes later, I was dressed. My imaginary stopwatch clocked in at forty minutes. That was a personal best.

My feet were bare, but I didn't care. Socks could be skipped. I spent enough time putting the necessary clothing on. No need to torture myself any further.

Forget about hair and makeup. I ran a brush through my hair to comb out the knots and called it a day. My hairdryer had been on hiatus for two weeks and would still be on vacation for another month.

My attire and appearance vastly differed from the dresses and full-on hair and makeup that I usually wore to work. I missed my heels, but in all reality, they probably couldn't support my broken back. I remembered high school Physics where we learned about pounds of pressure on a spiked heel...

I spent the rest of the day in the confines of the living room and kitchen.

I had yet to tackle the stairs to the second floor.

Chapter 12

Kindness of Others

After spending a few days at Dave's, he brought me back to my house with Charlotte and my tactical gear in tow.

I hadn't seen Anita in over a week, because she was with her dad, and I was excited to see her. She'd be home in a few hours.

After I pulled myself out of his car using the yank and twist routine, Dave cupped my elbow and helped me climb the three steps from the sidewalk to my front door. I had tackled a couple of simulated stairs at the rehab hospital but this was the first time I faced real ones because I never needed to go upstairs in his house. And without a handrail. Who knew that doing everyday tasks could be so arduous? I didn't envy the folks who permanently dealt with this. They had incredible strength, physically and mentally. I was fortunate that my condition was only temporary.

Wounded but not Dead

We stepped inside my house to find get-well cards and small vases of flowers that my parents had displayed from well-wishers. I sorted through the cards to see who sent them and saw many names of people with whom I had lost touch over the years. My heart melted. These people wanted to reach out to me to make sure I was okay. News about my accident traveled fast in our small town.

Dave opened my fridge to takeout containers full of dinners for the upcoming week.

"Look at all that food," he exclaimed.

"That's from Anita's field hockey team families," I told him. A week earlier, one mom had emailed me and said she wanted to ask other parents to volunteer to make dinners for Anita and me so that neither of us would have to cook. My fridge was full of pasta, soups, homemade macaroni and cheese, and roasted vegetables. A couple of packs of rolls were left on the counter.

"That was kind of them," he said.

"Yes, I know," I replied. "One less thing for me to worry about." Anita now knew she had to feed the dog, let her out, and do other obligatory things that I did like washing dishes and picking up around the house.

The only necessary thing I needed to do was get myself up and dressed. Everything else could wait. As a single mom, I was used to taking care of everything around our house. I couldn't stress about if Anita didn't do things exactly how I did them, the only thing that mattered was that it was done.

* * *

A few hours later, Anita came home from her dad's. She hugged me so hard she almost squeezed the stuffing out of me. The pain in my back was worth it. I hung out with her in the kitchen while she prepared our dinner. Afterward, she walked Charlotte, carried laundry upstairs for me, and did her homework.

Chapter 13

Backseat Driver

"Mom, I totally get it, but you need to chill," Anita warned me a few days later as she drove around town. I wanted to get out of the house and she had her eyes set on the mall. I grabbed my cane and settled into the front passenger seat of my other car.

Anita had her driver's permit. We also had my 2004 Honda Civic that Adam had been driving when he was home from college. If we didn't have both, she and I would have been stuck in the house and probably would have killed each other.

Despite having her permit for three months, she hadn't mastered deceleration or maintaining a safe distance between her and the car in front of us. As she crept a little too close to the car ahead of her, I shrieked, shielding my face with my arms.

"Slow down! Slow down! Slow down!"

"Mom!" Anita admonished me. "I get that you were in an accident, but if you freak out, then I will freak out and I might crash." For sixteen years old, she was wise beyond her years to grasp what I was going through.

"I'm sorry, I'm sorry," I told her, as I discreetly clenched my fists in fear. Flashbacks of my accident blazed in front of me. "I'll be better. I promise."

I had to trust her not to wreck the car. She was my main chauffeur until Dr. Bollinger cleared me to drive again.

When we arrived at the mall ten minutes later, I pulled myself out of the low-riding Civic with the yank and twist routine I had mastered. Anita was forced to slow her pace as I hobbled through the parking lot with my cane.

Once we wandered through the anchor store and into the main hallway, my overconfidence got the best of me. I was tired already. How could this be? Our mall wasn't that big. We affectionately called it 'The Small' because patrons could see from one end to the other.

"You go ahead and shop," I told Anita. Before my accident, we'd go into the stores together looking at outfits she wanted me to buy for her. Fortunately, my teenage daughter thought I had good taste. "I want to sit down and rest." Much to my dismay, the hard-backed benches were several hundred feet away toward the center of the mall. The firm benches made it easier for me to sit on without slouching my back.

Sighing, I settled into one of the complimentary overstuffed couches occupied by men holding bags for their wives who were in other stores. Anita might have to pull me out of it when we wanted to go home.

"Okay, Mom."

I handed her some cash and she was off.

* * *

Two weeks later, my friend Denise picked me up in her Jeep Rubicon to go out to dinner. She and I had been great friends for the past ten years and we had a standing monthly dinner date. Her vehicle proved to be a challenge for me. Namely, Rubicons are high off the ground and not comfortable for the vertically challenged like myself. Secondly, they don't usually have running boards. Denise's did not.

How would I get into her Jeep without twisting my back?

Hoping (praying!) that I didn't fall in the process, I grabbed her overhead hand strap and yanked myself upward into the vehicle.

"I'm so sorry!" Denise shrieked as she witnessed me using my strong biceps to pull myself into her car. "I didn't even think about it. I should have brought my other car."

Mental head slap.

Chapter 14

A New Normal

On Mondays, Wednesdays, and Thursdays for the next six weeks, I went to outpatient physical and occupational therapy. Dave dropped me off on the way to work. Sometimes Paul or Allan took me on their lunch breaks or I hailed an Uber. Even though I couldn't wait to drive myself again so that I didn't have to rely on others, I was simultaneously nervous to get back on the road.

The PTs had me walking on a treadmill, repping light weights, practicing my balance, and using a therapy band to stretch my core muscles. Despite my broken back, I was in decent shape and they pushed me.

At each therapy session, the OTs unwrapped my soft cast and plunged my broken hand into an incubator full of hot crushed corn pellets for 10 minutes. Yes, corn pellets. Someone, somewhere discovered the soothing sensation to help patients and it skyrocketed. I guess effective things don't always have to be high-tech.

The OTs also gave me different-strength hand grips to build up my muscles again. We sat together for a good hour each time and learned quite a lot about each other. Turns out, she used to work with my good friend Michele. Small world.

Despite the misconception of being satanic bastards for the pain they caused, the PT therapists were similarly welcoming. While I worked out, we chit-chatted about our personal lives. The one woman's son was in the same class as Anita. They all heard about my upcoming wedding and wanted to see pictures of my dress.

Dave and I postponed the wedding to January 26th. Physically, I felt good, but no way would I wear a back brace on my wedding day. I didn't consider myself a bridezilla but the brace over my wedding dress was non-negotiable. To our good fortune, the reception hall moved the date without charging us extra. Apparently, few people get married in January in Pennsylvania.

I had stopped taking any kind of pain medication by the end of October - less than a month after the accident. I didn't even need Tylenol. Sometimes my back flared up, but I dealt with the temporary pain with a heating pad - or bit on a bullet like they did in the Civil War. I'm kidding!

I also ditched my cane and mastered the stairs without bending my back. Freedom was in sight!

At home, I learned to improvise everyday tasks. I wasn't allowed to lift anything heavier than a gallon of milk nor bend my back at all. If my laundry basket was full and needed to be taken downstairs to the washer, I grabbed the handle and thunked it down the steps behind me. In the laundry room, I knelt in front of the washer and dryer and used my long-handled grabber to pull each article of clothing out of the washer and into the dryer one by one. The slow-going process took about 10 minutes, but I was glad I could do it without help.

I still relied on Anita and Dave to do a lot for me. They lifted heavy pots and carried clean laundry baskets back upstairs. I hated that they helped me, so I tried to minimize their efforts as much as possible. Swallowing my pride and asking for help was tough.

Emptying the dishwasher was the worst. Not only did I have to bend down on the floor, but I also had to kneel at an angle because the dishwasher door was in my way. I pulled each dish from the rack one by one and stacked them on the counter. After that slow process, I carried small groups of the dishes and put them in the upper cabinets. Back and forth. Up and down. Back and forth again. Who knew that doing something so mundane required so much effort?

With the assistance of my long-handled grabber, I could pick things up off the floor. The only time I struggled was when I dropped a pen and couldn't grasp it between the pinchers. I either left it on the floor or took the time to kneel down and pick it up. Oh, how I wished to be back to normal.

I spent most days in leggings and long-sleeved t-shirts with my back brace wrapped around my waist. Simple tasks like brushing my teeth and putting on shoes took great effort to not bend or twist my back. Occasionally, I treated myself to baggy jeans and a sweater when I went out with Anita or Dave.

The dinners from the field hockey parents had run out so I commandeered cooking for us again. Fortunately, I love to cook so I didn't mind the extra time that it took doing one thing at a time.

During the first few weeks home, I couldn't walk Charlotte and she was itching to go outside on the leash. One time I accidentally jingled Charlotte's collar on the hook near the front door and her ears perked up in dog memory muscle as if she knew we were going out. "Sorry, Charlotte, I didn't mean to get you excited," I told her. Defeated, she slunk away, probably cursing at me in doggie swear words under her breath.

As the days went on and I gained my strength, one day I pulled her collar and leash off the hook. She heard the noise from upstairs and bolted down the steps in seconds.

"Are you ready for this?" I asked her. Of course, she was, she had been waiting for this day for a month. But I wasn't sure if I could do it.

After I clipped everything to her and shrugged into a jacket, we went outside and headed for the sidewalk. Before my accident, we logged a mile every day. I knew I wasn't ready for that yet. Even though I didn't need my cane anymore, I still walked pretty slow and Charlotte wasn't used to my pace. We only went around the block and I was out of breath. Even though my body wasn't anywhere close to being back to normal, I was still thankful that I could take her for a walk.

The next day, Charlotte and I extended our route to two blocks. The day after that, we did three.

Chapter 15

Adam Came Home

At Thanksgiving break, Adam finally came home from college and saw me for the first time since my car accident. His girlfriend, Sandy, drove him home. They had been dating for a year and I often told him how lucky he was to have her. She was kind, smart, and sweet, and didn't put up with his teenage boy nonsense. When they came in the door, they squeezed me so hard. My back was getting stronger and I didn't have to fight through the pain.

"How are you feeling?" Adam asked me.

"Good most days," I told him. "But there's only so much I can do with a brace around my back all day."

"You look good though." Sandy beamed at me.

"Do you two want to go out for lunch?" I asked them. "I'll buy if you drive." I would have bought anyway, but I still needed others to chauffeur me around. Adam and Sandy were definitely getting the better end of the deal.

"Yes," Adam said. "I'm craving a good cheesesteak." We lived a good two hours away from Philadelphia, home of Tony Luke's Old Philly Style Sandwiches, but our local joint was almost as good. Almost.

We walked out the front door and down the steps to the sidewalk to Sandy's car. An early snowstorm had blown into town a few days before. The plowed streets and sidewalks made it easy to maneuver around town but white still completely covered the grass.

I successfully descended the stairs and shuffled along the sidewalk. One moment I was walking and --BAM!-- the next I was sitting on the snowy grass. I landed right on my tailbone.

Fortunately, I didn't feel any pain, not even through my snow-soaked jeans. I hoped it was a good sign.

"Mom!" Adam shrieked and immediately attempted to yank me forward up by my hands.

"No, don't," I told him, holding out my palm in a stop signal. If he continued the directional path of what he was doing, he surely would have caused me to bend my back. That was still a big no-no. The back brace kept my spine straight in the fall. Thank goodness for small miracles. "Go around me and lift me straight up from behind."

Adam skirted around me, put his arms under my armpits, and lifted me straight upward. Once I was standing, I reached behind me and placed a hand on my lower back under my brace. Nothing felt out of place. No pain surged through me.

"Do you think you're okay?" Sandy asked me.

"Yes, I think so," I replied.

"We'll take you to urgent care if you want to go," Adam offered.

I puffed out a deep breath.

"I think I'm fine," I told them. "Nothing hurts. I'll watch it for the next few hours and see."

I didn't want to scare my son, but panic raced through me. Under normal circumstances, I probably would have hurt nothing but my pride. But this time I feared I jammed my fragile vertebrae and undid all of the healing that I accomplished in the past six weeks.

The next few hours were deemed successful. My back was a little sore, but still not painful. I exhaled in relief. Six weeks had passed since my car accident. Dr. Bollinger told me in the hospital that I needed to wear the back brace for six to twelve weeks. I had already fought my way to within sight of freedom and I didn't want to go backward.

A few days later, Adam drove me to my follow-up appointment for my broken hand.

After Dr. Bogdan took a new x-ray, she gave me the good news. My hand was healed and I no longer had to wear the splint or do Occupational Therapy. Woo Hoo!

My follow-up appointment with Dr. Bollinger was in a couple of weeks. Hopefully, he would give me similar good news about my back.

Chapter 16

A Car Without a Driver

Dave said to me a few days before Thanksgiving, "We need to go buy you a new car."

"But I can't even drive it home yet," I protested. "Why bother?"

"Because it's the end of the month and almost the end of the year and we should be able to get you a good deal," he countered.

"Good point." Driving again scared the hell out of me, but I knew at some point I'd have to get back on the road. We did not live in a walkable city and public transportation was sketchy, so driving myself was my best option.

"Where do you want to look? Acura? BMW? Audi?" Dave asked me. He had been a BMW lover for several years.

"Honda."

"Honda?" He arched an eyebrow at me.

"Yes," I replied, unwavering. "I could have any car I want, but a Honda saved my life. Another car is not an option. I want a CR-V again."

Dave realized he wouldn't sway me. "Okay, let's go to the Honda dealership."

Fifteen minutes later, we sauntered into the Honda car lot and eyed up new CR-Vs. A salesman wearing a navy blue golf shirt with the dealership insignia stitched on his chest approached us.

"Hi, I'm Corey. You like the CR-Vs?" he asked us in more of a statement than a question.

"Yes, it saved my life," I answered, probably telling him more than what he wanted to know.

Corey lifted a brow. "Really? How's that?"

"I was in a car accident last month and broke my back." Unzipping my jacket, I presented the back brace around my waist. "I totaled my old CR-V but it stayed intact for the most part."

Pulling my phone out of my pocket, I showed him the photo of the accident scene from the local police website.

"Oh my god!" Corey cupped his mouth with his hand. That was the usual reaction I encountered when anyone saw the picture. "Can I use it to show others?"

"Yes, of course." Since the photo was taken by the police and considered public information, it didn't conflict with my lawsuit.

"Wow, I can't believe you're standing here now," he said, eyeing up my progress.

"Me either," Dave interjected. "She's a walking miracle."

We spent the next hour perusing new CR-Vs. In the three years that passed since I bought my last one, Honda added a few features like Lane Keep Assist and Blind Spot Warnings on both sides of the vehicle. My beloved side camera was gone but I'd make do.

The next day, Dave and I huddled at Corey's desk as I signed the paperwork for a new 2018 CR-V. I treated myself to the leather package, only because I was tired of Charlotte's fur needling into the fabric of my old car.

"But I still can't drive it home," I told them.

"Could you drop it off at the house?" Dave asked Corey.

"Yes, I can," Corey replied. "But it will probably be next week. Is that okay?"

I eyed my back brace that wrapped around my stomach and shrugged. "I'm not going anywhere between now and then."

A week later, Corey and one of his co-workers dropped off my new car. It sat in front of my house, taunting me.

Chapter 17

Freedom

On December 4th, two months to the day of my car accident, my friend Jackie drove me to Dr. Bollinger's office. She worked part-time and my doctor's appointment fell on her day off. Jackie stayed behind in the waiting room while I went into Dr. Bollinger's private office.

"I took a look at your x-rays from last week and everything has healed nicely. You look great!" Dr. Bollinger told me as I took a seat across from him. His large oak desk separated us.

"Thank you." I blushed.

"How's your pain level?" he asked me.

"Like a one or two most days." I flicked my hand in front of him. "Nothing too painful but enough to tell me it's there."

"Okay that's good," he replied. "Do you need a refill on your pain medication?"

"No."

"No?" Dr. Bollinger arched an eyebrow at me.

"Why would I?" I glared at him like he had three heads. "I haven't taken any kind of pain medication since October 29th."

"You're kidding? That's was five weeks ago," he deduced.

"I know," I confirmed.

"That's fantastic!" He beamed at me like I was his opus. "Most of my patients come in here and tell me they ran out well before I can prescribe more and I have to tell them no." He didn't want me to be like Ryan O'Callaghan, a former NFL player, who openly admitted to refilling his pain medications nine times in one month after shoulder surgery.

"I haven't even taken anything over the counter either," I told him. "No Tylenol. No ibuprofen. Nothing."

"Wow, that's great." Dr. Bollinger waved his hand at me as a motion for me to stand up. "I want you to take off your brace now."

"What?" I blinked in disbelief. "You're serious?" Even though I hadn't taken any medicine for over a month, I used my back brace as a crutch. It helped me when I fell on the ice a couple of weeks earlier. I was terrified to move my back for fear of damaging the fragile bones, but I rose from my chair as instructed.

"Yes, I'm serious," he replied. "Your x-rays from last week look great. Your back is completely healed. If you injure yourself again anytime soon, you won't hurt your back. It's solid now with the rods and pins."

"But..." Even though the evidence proved otherwise, I still didn't believe him. "Are you sure?"

"Yes, I'm sure," he replied.

Puffing out a hesitant breath, I slowly undid my weighty back brace. The Velcro pulled apart, opening the doors to my freedom. I had depended on the brace for the past two months; my medicinal crutch. I laid it on the chair next to me. The feeling without it was liberating, yet petrifying. That brace had become part of my daily life for the past two months. I didn't know what I could do without it.

"How do you feel?" Dr. Bollinger asked me.

"About 10 pounds lighter," I joked. "And I'll be able to put my shoes on without squatting on the stairs."

Dr. Bollinger laughed.

"Now I want you to bend toward your toes," he instructed. "Slowly."

I took a deep breath and bent my core forward, inch by inch. I stopped, waiting for something to pop or shift inside me.

"Keep going," he said. "Bend as far as you can go. Your body has pushed itself to get better. It's not like cancer cells are fighting back."

I bent my body even further, almost to a 60-degree angle, but I could no longer touch my toes like I used to because of the unforgiving hardware in my back. Nothing inside me moved or crackled.

"How do you feel now?" Dr. Bollinger wanted to know.

"Good, but are you sure this is okay?" I wondered from my arched position.

"Yes, I'm sure," he chuckled. Of course, he was sure; he was the doctor. "Now stand upright again."

I did as instructed like I was playing Simon Says.

"You're done wearing that brace," he told me.

"Forever?" I was still unconvinced that I was healed.

"Forever."

"Does this mean I can drive again too?" I asked him.

"Yes," Dr. Bollinger replied.

I had never heard more beautiful words. I knew once he cleared me to drive, that I was almost new again. Except for the rods and screws in my back for the rest of my life.

"You're a miracle worker," I told him.

"Just doing my job," he sheepishly grinned. "You did all the work with your therapy."

"Speaking of that," I said, "how much longer do I have to go? And when can I go back to work?"

"You need to keep going to your PT sessions for at least a few more weeks," he said. "I'll have them evaluate you then and they'll be able to determine how much longer you need to go. I suspect they'll release you based on what I see now, but they will determine that, not me. You can go to work soon after that. Days even."

I quickly did the math in my head. "I could be done with physical therapy by the end of the month and go back to work at the beginning of January?"

"Yes, it's highly possible," he told me. "You've come a long way in such a short time. Most patients with back injuries like yours are still using walkers or canes at this stage."

Part of me was thankful that I was leaps and bounds ahead of other patients. The other part empathized with them. If I could sit with any of them, I'd tell them that they need to push through and not take the easy way out; that they don't have to accept their fate if they don't want it.

"Does this mean I won't be seeing you anymore?" I asked him.

"Not unless you break your back again." Dr. Bollinger grinned.

With that, I left him in his office and headed to the waiting room, dragging my back brace in my hand behind me.

"Look at you!" Jackie eyed up my brace-free waist.

"I know! I'm so happy! No more brace." I beamed wide at her as she gave me a huge hug, now knowing she couldn't break me.

"You're completely healed?" she asked me while releasing me.

"Yep," I said. "I have to go to Physical Therapy for a few more weeks and then I can probably go back to work in a month. And... I can drive again!"

"That's great news!" Jackie replied. "I'm so happy for you."

Me too, Jackie, me too.

Chapter 18

Reliving Driver's Ed

Once again, Dave proved to me what a godsend he was. I couldn't wait to marry this man.

"You can do this," he encouraged me as I sat in the driver's seat of my new Honda CR-V. He settled next to me in the passenger seat.

Jolts of panic surged through me, tensing my body. My white knuckles clenched the steering wheel. My stomach bound itself into a hundred knots. A rapid pulse pounded my temple.

I hadn't driven a car in over two months. Not only was I out of practice, but the last time I drove, I wound up in intensive care for three days.

Driving again terrified me.

"Let's take it slow," Dave cheered me on. "You can do this."

Turning the engine on, I gulped in a deep breath. I put the car in reverse and backed out of the driveway at a snail's pace. A moment later, we stopped in the middle of the street in front of the house.

"Okay, I did it, I'm done," I told Dave. Until now, my recovery had been uneventful. In the hospital, I had a few days of excruciating pain where I wanted to curl up and die, but ever since then, my body decided not to mutiny.

"Nice try," he countered. "Now put it in drive and we'll go around the block."

"What if I don't want to?" I parried.

"Babe," Dave cooed at me. "You have to do this. You can't not drive."

"Sure I can," I replied. I hadn't thought it through, but I had to come up with any excuse not to drive. I needed to steam clean the carpets. I needed to floss Charlotte's teeth. I needed to rearrange the basement.

"You can do this," Dave repeated. "I know you can. You've come this far. And Dr. Bollinger told you that you are leaps and bounds above most people with your injuries. You're a fighter. I won't let you give up now."

Dave was right. I had to push through my fear of driving again. He was always there for me, even when I didn't think I needed it.

I puffed out a long breath and put the car in drive. Hesitantly, I pushed my foot on the gas pedal and the car inched forward. A turtle moved faster. Gradually, I made my way down the street, around the block, and through the neighborhood.

Another car approached me at the next intersection. Like a teenager learning to drive for the first time, I waved the other car through knowing that I would be going slower.

I drove Dave through a few more streets going 15 miles per hour and then we wound up back at the house.

"You did it!" he cheered me on. "Put it in park and we'll do more tomorrow."

"But I'm nowhere near ready to go on a major road," I told him.

"I know," he said. "But you'll get there. And I'll help you."

His optimism made me smile.

The following week, I drove myself to physical therapy for the first time. What a liberating feeling! I didn't have to rely on my friends to take me or spend money on Uber. To my good fortune, the outpatient center was not on a major highway and I could drive side streets to get to it. I still wasn't ready to tackle traffic or speeds above 35. I was aware of every vehicle near me. Regardless of being on a residential street, I still stayed far behind any truck or van carrying cargo. My Lane Keep Assist control in my new car often barked at me when I hugged the white line when other cars came at me in the oncoming lane.

Driving terrified me. But each day I drove gave me more confidence than the day before.

Baby steps.

Chapter 19

Back to Work

By the end of December, my physical therapist cleared me and gave me at-home exercises to do every day. Mentally and physically, I was ready to go back to work.

One afternoon, Anita came home from school and found me in the kitchen stirring up a DIY concoction. She said, "Mom, you must be pretty bored at home if you're making soap."

My driving had progressed too. I had graduated from side streets to major roads and topped my speed at 65, but I still hadn't driven in rush hour traffic. Being at home had its perks. I didn't have to get up at 5:45 to go to work in the morning.

On January 2nd, almost three months after my accident, I finally went back to work. That morning, I put makeup on and blow-dried my hair, things I hadn't done in three months. I pulled on trousers and a blouse, opposite of my jeans and sweaters that had been a staple in my wardrobe all winter.

With my packed lunch next to me in my car, I was ready to go. My body tensed with anxiety. The last time I drove this route, I was inches and seconds away from dying. I took a right on the main road, heading out of the downtown historic section. To my right, the mutilated telephone pole tormented me; its sides still gashed out from when I slammed into it. Like me, it still stood erect, even with a few deformities.

I expelled a sigh of relief as I made my way around the ill-fated S-curve without complications. I hummed along the one-lane main road to the highway ramp a couple of miles away. On the highway, I stayed in the right lane chugging along at 55 miles per hour, not caring if other drivers swerved around me doing 70. I wasn't taking any chances. Stop-and-go traffic weaved in and out of the three lanes surrounding me.

All the reasons to not keep going forward consumed me. I could easily take the next exit ramp and go back home, along the side streets. No one would miss me. If I could have peeled my white-knuckled hands off the steering wheel, I would have bitten my nails right off like a famished squirrel.

More cars and trucks whizzed past me. A white utility van hauling ladders on the roof merged into the space in front of me.

Holy crap.

What if those ladders came undone? What if they flew right through my windshield? What if...?

The white van crept forward as I decelerated, creating more space between us. I exhaled in relief.

A few minutes later, I took the exit ramp for downtown and integrated into city traffic. Traffic lights in every block discourage vehicles from speeding. I was safe behind several cars at an intersection. Then, from the crossroads, a tractor-trailer attempted to make a right turn onto our street. As it missed the first car by mere inches, I jumped in my seat, trapped within a steel frame. I couldn't breathe, as if something was trying to choke me.

I still had a half-mile to go. What would I do?

Somehow I found my way to the parking lot, still shaking from the drive. There had to be another way to get to work every day. I couldn't put myself through this again. Once parked, I stood outside my car and inhaled a few deep breaths trying to calm myself.

After a few moments of serenity, I left the parking lot and walked toward my building.

Inside, my co-worker, Sam, was coming to work at the same time and she rode up the elevator with me. We 'lived' on the 3rd floor of a 16 story building. Before my accident, I religiously walked the stairs every morning to our floor. That morning, I wasn't ready to tackle them.

As Sam and I departed the elevator, we wound our way around the cube-farm to our desks. She sat two spaces over from me.

"Who's birthday was it last week?" I asked her, pointing to the group of balloons hovering over the middle of the top of the cube walls.

"No one's," she said as we walked closer to our desks.

"Oh wait," I giggled, "they're for me." Someone had filled my cube with neon-colored streamers and a matching banner that said: "Welcome Back".

"Did you know about this?" I asked Sam.

She shook her head. "But we're glad you're back. You look great."

Throughout the day, my coworkers tightly hugged me and welcomed me back. One man nearly cried in his embrace because he was so thankful I was alive.

After eight hours at work, I went home and promptly fell asleep on the couch, exhausted. Who knew being a desk jockey could be so tiring?

* * *

A week later, while I was getting dressed for work, I reached for the black stacked heels that I wore on the day of my car accident. They had patiently waited for me to put them on again. But I still couldn't bring myself to wear the cursed pink and black boho skirt from that fateful day.

As I sat down to strap a shoe on (because the rods and pins in my back prevented me from standing and putting shoes on at the same time), the two-inch heel flapped back and forth in my hand.

That's odd. How did it break? I hadn't worn them in over three months.

The only explanation that I could come up with was that my shoe broke during the collision. Maybe I slammed my foot down or unknowingly bent it on a hard angle while trying to control my car?

A pair of shoes was a minor sacrifice in the grand scheme of things. The collateral damage could have been a lot worse.

Chapter 20

Hit the Panic Button

A few weekends later, after I settled into a new routine of going to work every morning, I headed out to run some errands on a Sunday afternoon. Traffic was light, with a few local motorists going in and out of my town. I followed a white sedan along Main Street and we both made a right turn onto the road that would lead me to the store.

As we crossed the railroad tracks on the north end of town, a flatbed truck pulled onto the road in front of the white sedan.

Holy crap!

The truck was hauling granite slabs and came from the same company that the truck from my accident was headed that fateful day. The slabs were arranged upward like an A-frame, exactly like the truck from my accident. Was this one also carrying 14 tons? Was it strapped correctly? Would these granite slabs fall off too?

My heart thumped like a jackhammer inside me. The white sedan provided a soothing buffer between the truck and me. If any granite fell from the truck, it would most likely hit the white sedan and not me. That thought gave me some comfort. I exhaled in relief.

The white sedan leisurely made its way along two more blocks then stopped and put its left turn signal on waiting for cross traffic to create a vacancy. I contentedly waited behind it. The flatbed truck ahead of us was gaining distance and I had no desire to get anywhere near it. I had another two miles to go and hoped that I would never reach the flatbed truck.

A few moments later, the white sedan made the intended left turn and I went on my way. For the next mile, I had the whole road to myself. The flatbed truck was nowhere in sight. Maybe it turned onto another road?

As I made my way around a blind bend in the road, I slammed on my brakes almost coming nose-to-end with the flatbed truck. My white knuckles clenched the steering wheel, as I tried to stay in the path of the two-lane road without hitting oncoming traffic or ending up in the ditch. All of my fears fell out of me into a mental free-fall. Would I succumb to the same fate? Would I be as lucky this time? Or dead? My thoughts jumbled together into a hard knot.

I decelerated creating more space between my car and the truck. I couldn't release my hands from the steering wheel to rub out the tension in my temple. Everything was spinning around me while I desperately tried to control my car. My body quaked in response. My ribs heaved in and out as if bound by ropes, straining to inflate my lungs. I couldn't stop though. I had a half-mile to go. Somehow, in a trance, I continued driving.

Less than a minute later, the flatbed truck stopped at a red light at the next intersection. I stopped as well, but a good 100 feet behind it. No way would I get anywhere near that load of granite. Not if I could help it. My breathing slowed; my destination was in sight.

While I waited for the light to turn green, I fumbled for my phone in my bag to snap a picture of the truck in front of me. For the past three and a half months, I described the truck coming at me from my accident. No one, not even Dave, could visualize what I saw that ominous day. Until now.

When the light turned green, the flatbed truck accelerated and continued down the road. I made the next right 100 yards ahead into the shopping plaza and parked. Finally, I peeled my hands from the steering wheel and gulped in hefty pockets of air. Half of my brain told me I was okay. The other half wanted to take off running and never drive again.

I picked up my phone again and called Dave.

"Hi," I breathed into the phone.

"What's wrong? Are you okay?" He must have picked up on my panicked tone.

"I'm physically fine," I puffed out. "I just saw another truck carrying a load of granite."

"Holy crap! Are you okay?" Dave repeated.

"I can't do this," I told him. "I can't drive. I'm scared to death."

"Yes, you can," he said. "Yes, you can. I know you can."

Admitting I was nervous to drive made me ashamed. Until then, humor helped me deflect my anxiety. Everyone else could drive; I feared it. How could I be so scared when it felt second nature to everyone around me?

To be independent again, I had to push through my fear. I had to.

Chapter 21

Winter Wedding

A week before our wedding date, Dave and I headed to the county courthouse to get a new marriage license. We both worked a few blocks away so we made the trek on a cold January afternoon on our lunch break.

"You two were in here before, weren't you?" the brunette clerk questioned us at the counter. "I think I remember you."

"Yes, we were," I replied. "Our other license expired last month."

"She was in a bad car accident and we postponed the wedding," Dave said to the clerk and pointed to me. "We're getting married next week."

"That way if we have to postpone again, we have some time," I joked. A Pennsylvania marriage license has a lifespan of 60 days.

"Oh wow, I'm so sorry," the bubbly clerk exclaimed. "When a marriage license expires, it usually means the wedding was called off."

"No, not this time," Dave reassured her.

"Come with me and we'll fill out your paperwork again," she instructed. Dave and I followed her to her desk and we spent the next twenty minutes answering the necessary questions. Why on earth did the Commonwealth of Pennsylvania need to know what my mother's occupation was? At least they no longer required us to take a blood test or get a physical.

* * *

A week later, Dave and I were married on January 26, 2019.

Someone, somewhere blessed us with great weather for the middle of winter in Pennsylvania. The sun shone and no precipitation fell from the sky. This time of year meant lifeless clouds and a concoction of snow, wind, and rain. Temps of 35 degrees made it unusually balmy. Our photographer snapped a few photos outside before the sun set.

My mom had been diligently working on my wedding dress since my car accident. I wanted something simple: luxurious fabric in a classic sheath akin to Carolyn Bessette when she married John F. Kennedy Jr. in 1996. My mom questioned the deep V back, saying it would expose my scars. I insisted on the design, proud of my wounds. They were now part of me and I had no reason to hide them. They reminded me that I was still breathing.

Dave and I invited 50 of our closest friends and family. My cousins and aunt drove in from Pittsburgh. Dave's cousins and my best friend traveled from Connecticut. My younger brother flew in from Florida. No one declined the wedding invitation. I think everyone was anxious and thankful for some happy news in our life.

Our ceremony was held in the rotunda of the Pennsylvania Capitol Building, a Beaux-Arts style with decorative Renaissance themes throughout. Almost like the Sistine Chapel, the rotunda ceiling displayed detailed artwork adorned with gold trim framing. On October 4, 1906 (112 years to the day before my car accident), then-President Teddy Roosevelt dedicated it and proclaimed the new building, "the handsomest state capitol I have ever seen."

Dave and I kept the wedding simple: no bridal party, no tuxes, no matching dresses, no over-the-top centerpieces, no rehearsal dinner. I bought my bouquet of lilies and roses at the local street vendor for $25. My cousin's son provided music with his piano and guitar-playing prowess.

Adam and my dad escorted me down the two stories of steep steps of the rotunda where Dave stood below. At first, I fought them, insisting I could descend the stairs myself. But once I disembarked the first few aged steps of the grandiose staircase and tottered in my four-inch heels, I was thankful for their reinforcements.

Dave rattled through his vows with confidence and grace. Like he did with everything else.

When it was my turn, I only made it through the first sentence and then I bawled like a baby. My emotions knocked me over. The combination of jubilation, solace, and timidity that I had been experiencing for the past few months enveloped me. Dave had been a godsend throughout and I was thankful and lucky that I could marry him. When he proposed, little did he know he would have to endure "in sickness and in health" so soon.

At the reception, our friends and family mingled at a historic 18th-century tavern that had been converted to a large restaurant. We dined on hors d'oeuvres while listening to my cousin's son sing and play his guitar.

An hour in, I gathered everyone together to hear my son's speech.

Adam spoke:

"This afternoon, we are sitting around at lunch talking about some funny stories about Dave and my mom. For example, in the span of 18 months, Dave got 17 parking tickets, and each parking ticket is around $30, so that's around $500 that Dave basically threw down the crapper. So then my mom got a parking ticket last summer and she tried to tell us it was Dave's fault she got the ticket. I'll let you guys be the judge... What happened was they were meeting for drinks somewhere after work, and she left her spot that she doesn't have to pay for, to get a little closer to the bar. She parked at 4:15 and the meter maids stop ticketing for parking at 5:00. Dave told her that she was fine not to put coins in the meter because they never check. My mom and Dave walked back to the car around 5:15 and there my mom sees a parking ticket on her window marked for 4:51, only nine minutes before the meter maids stop checking. She then continued to say it was Dave's fault and it wouldn't have happened if she would have paid the $3 meter fee. I don't know about you guys, but I'm not sure I would have trusted the guy who got a parking ticket every month for 18 months, but that's me.

For those of you who don't know, my mom has two cultural backgrounds, the Italian side from her mom, which is known for being tan and loving wine, and the tougher Irish background from her dad. Now my mom only shows one side of the Italian stereotype considering it only takes about five minutes in the sun before she starts to develop the nice red glow of a tomato. No wonder she chased me around as a kid asking me if I put sunscreen on every five minutes. (This is true.) Continuing with the Irish side, my mom is the model for toughness. In fact, her last name says just this. Here is a little bit of a history lesson for you on the background of my mom's maiden name. The last name Walsh has a fairly well-known family crest in Irish culture. On top of the crest, an image depicts a swan pierced with an arrow on top of the helmet of a knight. Under the crest is the family motto. Family mottos were often used as war cries when anyone in the family was going into battle. What this motto says is 'Transfixus sed non Mortuus'. For those of you who aren't fluent in Latin, that means 'Wounded but not Dead'. The Irish Catholics were persecuted throughout Europe, and Walsh was the last name of many Irish Catholics. The motto basically means that no matter what someone did to the family, it would only make them stronger. Now, you're probably wondering what this has anything to do with my mom and this wedding as a whole. If you didn't know, my mom was in a bad car accident in early October, where she suffered a few minor injuries and a fractured L3 vertebrae.

Most people don't recover from these types of back injuries for a long time, if at all. My mom isn't most people. She was up and walking a week after surgery, and she was cleared to drive again two months after the accident. If you ask me, that is the epitome of toughness. As for Dave, he was there with her every day in the hospital and was sending me daily updates, so for this, I thank him very much. I've seen firsthand the happiness that he brings my mom and it warms my heart to see my mom so happy again. Cheers!"

My eyes filled with happy tears. Adam's speech was a complete surprise. I couldn't be more proud of my son.

Chapter 22

Any Day Above Ground is a Great Day

I have titanium rods and screws in my back for the rest of my life, but I have nothing to complain about. So many other people have it worse than me. The veteran who lost her leg in Iraq. The man who endured hours of chemo.

Yes, I had to learn to walk again, but I am lucky and will always be blessed that nothing worse happened to me.

Since my car accident, I've never spent a more conscious time in my life. If my back gets tired from sitting and I need to stand for a while, I'm okay with that. That means I still have two legs to stand on. Sometimes I hesitate to descend steep stairs in old buildings, but then I grab the handrail and take them one by one.

If the barometric pressure changes when a rainstorm blows through, my back gets a little sore for a couple of hours. I can't slouch on a couch and need to put a stiff pillow behind me. But I will not complain.

If I drop something on the floor (and curse), I now have to bend my knees to reach down or get on my hands and knees to retrieve it instead of simply bending over like I used to. My back might not be 100% anymore and I can't do the things I used to do, but I'm okay with that. I gave away my skis and I probably shouldn't ice skate. But it's better than being taken away in a body bag.

I have a nice set of scars on my lower back. Sometimes they itch and drive me crazy, but they remind me that I'm here. I'm alive, and for that I'm indebted.

People in my town heard about my accident even though my name was never mentioned in the news article. One man I hadn't seen in two years came up to me and gave me a big hug. Everyone is shocked at how well I am doing and thankful that I wasn't hurt worse.

Every morning before work, I do two minutes of planks and strength training exercises to continue my at-home physical therapy. Some days I have zero interest in doing my training, but I know I have to in order to keep my body strong. Charlotte and I are back to walking over a mile. I take the stairs at work and try to hike all 16 floors a couple of times a week. I do these things because I don't want to be confined to a bed or wheelchair for the rest of my life.

Getting dressed requires the skills of an amateur contortionist. I can no longer stand on one leg and put my socks and shoes on. Instead, I have to sit on a chair and slowly bend like a 90-year-old man trying to put on his clothes.

I'm still terrified to drive. If a truck is in front of me, I'll maintain a good hundred feet between it and my car. If another vehicle wants to drive around me and get up on that truck's bumper, be my guest. I stay far behind every truck carrying lumber, every utility van hauling ladders, every semi transporting sewer pipes. PTSD will probably affect me for the rest of my life.

I push through every day driving to work because I have to. I can't let my fear conquer me. If Lijana Wallenda can get back on a highwire above Times Square after a devastating fall, I can certainly drive again.

Six months after my accident, my back surged with pain for several days. I hadn't been in this much pain since I was in the ICU. I called Dr. Bollinger and he told me to take some Tylenol and watch it for a couple more days. He wasn't sure what was causing the issue without looking at an x-ray. I probably couldn't get into the imaging center for another week so I decided to tough it out. My friend bought me an Icy-Hot patch for some relief. Within two days, my pain subsided. Who knows if that will happen again? If it does, I'll be prepared with another Icy-Hot patch and a call to Dr. Bollinger.

I marvel at all of the people who helped me: the strangers who pulled me from my car, the ER staff, the physical and occupational therapists. My friends and family drove me everywhere and gave me unconditional support and love. They made a traumatic experience easier to bear. I don't know how I could have gone through it alone.

Life is risk. I'm not in control the second I walk out that door. I think I am, but I'm not. I think I have a handle on any situation - but then 14 tons of granite pushes my car against a telephone pole, breaks my back, and I have to learn to walk again. I might get into another accident someday. Someone might attack me. I might fly in a plane that goes down or eat food that sends me to the ER. Anything can happen to me at any moment. I'll make plans like I'm in control, but I'm really not. None of us are in control of anything. I hope none of these things happen to me but all I can do is master my reaction and response. If I hadn't seen the granite falling off the truck in front of me and swerved to the side, I might not be here today.

Everyone feels sorry for me that I broke my back and learned to walk again. But they shouldn't be. I won't let this freak accident change my view of life. I'm here. I will continue to do what I'm doing. I'm still alive and, for that, I will be forever grateful.

# # #

Acknowledgments

I want to personally thank all of my family and the following friends who either came to visit me in the hospital or continually called or texted to see how I was doing:

Amy, Lisa, Josh, Paul, Lydia, Allan, Janna, Manju, Christi, Denise, Julie, Michele, Lizanne, Adeline, Sue, Tom, Sam, Niki, Kim, Shannyn, Kristin, Kelly, Eric, Helen, Chris, Robert, Jackie. (I hope I remembered everyone.) Your friendship and encouragement made a difficult time easier to bear.

To Dave - marrying you was the best decision I ever made.

Kristin wrote this to me at my one-year back-iversary:
"Wow, can't believe it's been a year. I'll never forget your text. I was so worried about you. I'm so glad you are here and so proud of you for everything you have gone through and accomplished this past year. It's so easy to look at you and forget because you look great. I know you still have some pain and discomfort and that you might not be able to touch your toes anymore, but I honestly don't know what I would have done if I lost you. So glad I still have you and that you are doing so well. You are strong and you will overcome the anxiety you sometimes have. I know you will. Love you!"

# # #

Wounded but not Dead

Thank you for reading my book.
If you enjoyed it, won't you please take a moment to leave me a
review at your favorite retailer?
One or two sentences are perfectly fine.
Help an author out. ☺
Thanks!

Want some cool merch from me?
Post a pic of this book on your social media and tag me!
@marywalshwrites
Tag me on:

**Sign up for my sometimes-monthly newsletter and
order autographed books at:**
marywalshwrites.com

Follow me on Goodreads and Amazon:
www.goodreads.com/goodreadscommarywalshwrites
www.amazon.com/author/marywalsh2

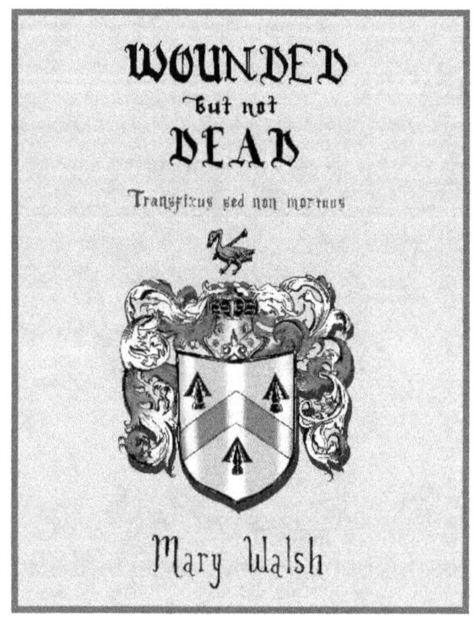

Illustration by Margarita Aleixo